PRAISE FOR *MAKING THINGS RIGHT AT WORK*

Culture drives results. And every team's culture rises and falls on its relationships. These three authors bring you actionable strategies for keeping your work relationships on track. If your team's productivity is hampered by relational struggles, this is the book for you.

MICHAEL HYATT
Wall Street Journal bestselling coauthor of *Win at Work & Succeed at Life*

As a nonprofit consultant and executive coach, I help leaders navigate conflict every day. And as we build more diverse workplaces, the need for tools to ensure that tension is healthy is exponentially greater. This is a smart, no-nonsense book with no jargon and terrific tools. Consider a copy for everyone on your team and use it for group discussion. That's my plan.

JOAN M. GARRY
Founder, Nonprofit Leadership Lab

Every business is people working with and leading people to do stuff for people. If every team read this field guide for healthier relationships, it would change people, thus changing business. This is practical, and workplaces around the world need this!

MIKE SHARROW
CEO of C12

Conflict is personal, so handling it well requires a personal approach. And that's exactly what incorporating the foundation of the five love languages does for conflict resolution in this brilliant work. Every workplace and organization should have a copy of this book!

MICHELLE MYERS

Founder of she works HIS way and coauthor of *She Works His Way: A Practical Guide for Doing What Matters Most in a Get-Things-Done World*

In order to have a healthy, thriving organization, the people within the organization must be aligned and thriving. Nothing breeds inefficiency and counterproductive behavior more than unhealthy, unresolved conflict. When conflict occurs—wherever it occurs—what does it look like to live out our core belief that people matter? I believe this is one of the most important conversations we should be having right now, not just at work, but in every area of our lives. This invaluable book provides the practical insight and strategies to not only understand conflict, but to navigate it well. It belongs in the hands of every leader I know!

MEREDITH KING

Executive director, Integrus leadership; author, *Immovable: Reflections to Build Your Life and Leadership on Solid Ground*

MAKING THINGS RIGHT
at *Work*

INCREASE TEAMWORK, RESOLVE CONFLICT, AND BUILD TRUST

Gary Chapman,
Jennifer Thomas
& Paul White

NORTHFIELD PUBLISHING
CHICAGO

Some content is adapted from material previously published online by Jennifer Thomas and Paul White.

Some names and details have been changed to protect the privacy of individuals, while some are fictitious or composites for the sake of illustration.

Edited by Elizabeth Cody Newenhuyse
Interior and cover design: Erik M. Peterson
Author photo of Gary Chapman: Grooters Productions
Author photo of Jennifer Thomas: Ross Thomas Photography
Author photo of Paul White: Michael Bankston

Library of Congress Cataloging-in-Publication Data

Names: Chapman, Gary D., 1938- author. | Thomas, Jennifer, 1969- author. | White, Paul E., 1957- author.
Title: Making things right at work : how to handle conflict and build trust / Gary Chapman, Jennifer Thomas, & Paul White.
Description: Chicago : Northfield Publishing, [2022] | Includes bibliographical references. | Summary: "Dr. Gary Chapman and business consultants Dr. Jennifer Thomas and Dr. Paul White offer strategies for restoring harmony at work. Don't let broken relationships taint your work environment. Take steps to make things right . . . not tomorrow, but today. The success of your career depends on it!"-- Provided by publisher.
Identifiers: LCCN 2021044631 (print) | LCCN 2021044632 (ebook) | ISBN 9780802422736 | ISBN 9780802499448 (ebook)
Subjects: LCSH: Conflict management. | Work environment. | Trust. | Interpersonal relations. | Quality of work life. | BISAC: BUSINESS & ECONOMICS / Workplace Culture | BUSINESS & ECONOMICS / Conflict Resolution & Mediation
Classification: LCC HM1126 .C45 2022 (print) | LCC HM1126 (ebook) | DDC 303.6/9--dc23
LC record available at https://lccn.loc.gov/2021044631
LC ebook record available at https://lccn.loc.gov/2021044632

We hope you enjoy this book from Northfield Publishing. Our goal is to provide high-quality, thought-provoking books and products that connect truth to your real needs and challenges. For more information on other books and products that will help you with all your important relationships, go to northfieldpublishing.com or write to:

Northfield Publishing
820 N. LaSalle Boulevard
Chicago, IL 60610

1 3 5 7 9 10 8 6 4 2

Printed in the United States of America

*To our children, and their children, all of whom deserve
a kinder, gentler, and less fractured world.*

CONTENTS

INTRODUCTION

AS WE WERE COMPLETING THIS manuscript, America was— very cautiously—"opening back up." Although conditions vary across the country, companies large and small are working on plans to bring back employees, at least on a "hybrid" basis. Some workers are looking forward to reconnecting. Others, not so much—because they have to work with other people, and wherever there are people, conflict follows.

Conflict at work happens—a lot. In fact, it shouldn't take you but a few seconds to recall a tense moment in your workplace. To relive the sting of a casual comment. To remember the discomfort of watching a not-so-friendly disagreement in a meeting. Or how about the resentment that simmered when a teammate dropped the ball on an important presentation you and he were doing—and didn't apologize?

The three of us, each in our own profession, have spent considerable time analyzing human behavior, studying workplace dynamics, listening and counseling, and researching the nature of apology and forgiveness. As society resets following the pandemic, many institutions, from schools to churches to businesses, are asking themselves: *What do we need to do better?*

Coping with conflict among colleagues is one of those "do-better" challenges. One study found that each employee spends (on average) 2.1 hours every week (or one day per month) dealing with some form of conflict. For the US alone, that adds up to 385 million working days a year devoted to coping with workplace conflict![1] Which means you're *not* doing something else—selling or producing or promoting or monitoring or fixing. Something that actually furthers the company's business.

Think about that.

On the other hand, effectively managing interpersonal issues *is* absolutely central to the organization's success. Situations that are left to fester can create low morale, impact productivity, and even drive valued employees to look for greener pastures. So the wise leader will utilize the variety of tools at his or her disposal to deal with conflict.

At a personal level, recalling conflictual situations we each have had in our working career doesn't take much effort. Here are a few examples:

- One of your team members is oddly distant in how they are relating to you recently. It is apparent they are upset with you about something, but you don't know why. You try to address the situation by asking them if you've done something to offend them, but they respond coolly, "No, everything's okay," and the conversation ends there.
- You feel angry and betrayed—stabbed in the back. You found out that Becky, one of your coworkers, told Kim (who supervises both of you) about tasks you are not completing on time and how you're not following procedures. Becky never talked to you directly about any of this.
- In a team Zoom meeting, you're blindsided by your supervisor—in front of others. You proposed an idea. She responded with what you interpreted as a condescending smile and said, "No, I don't think that is the way we should go. Anyone have a better idea?" And you felt as small as the thumbnail of your face on the screen.

- Your colleague Tim and your boss, Raj, get along quite well. They have mutual interests and frequently eat lunch together, talking about coaching their kids' sports. You (Stephanie) feel left out, partly because you are a woman and partly because you don't share similar interests. You believe Tim has undue influence on Raj and also receives special treatment (getting to leave early on Fridays to attend his daughter's games).

Yes, conflicts, disagreements, and misunderstandings are inevitable in the workplace. But how they are handled will make or break coworker relationships—creating either a healthy or toxic work environment. Our goal is to provide a framework for understanding relational difficulties at work and offer tools to manage them effectively. We do not believe that attempting to build a conflict-free workplace is realistic or even desirable. Differences—of perspective, in personality, in communication style, in values and priorities—are critical to building thriving organizations.

But too much conflict or "drama" can become toxic and a drain on managers' and workmates' time, and a hindrance to healthy functioning as an organization. Here we want to help you correctly understand disagreements and navigate relational challenges between coworkers. Our goal is to help you prevent or at least minimize the escalation of festering conflicts.

WHAT WE BELIEVE

In order to truly accept and apply the advice we will be giving, you must first understand the guiding principles we as authors and professionals hold regarding employees, leaders, work, and relationships.

Our foundational view of *employees* is to respect each person regardless of position: each employee has value as a person (beyond their production). We believe every person has inherent value for who they are, not just what they do. Therefore, everyone should be treated with dignity and respect. We believe there is something of value we can affirm in each person, regardless of their abilities, education, and experience.

Leaders, we believe, function best when they lead by considering the needs and desires of their customers and clients, the team members they are managing, and the organization they serve. Leading is more than telling others what to do. Leading is understanding the big picture of what the goals for the team are, organizing resources, and providing direction to accomplish those goals.

The *purpose of work* is not solely to make money, achieve status, or wield influence. Rather, the purpose of work is to provide the goods or services that others need (or want). From a business point of view, "and are willing to pay for them" needs to be added, but this is not always true in charitable work or ministry. From this perspective, "having a job" is not just about earning money but includes meeting the needs of others—either our employer or our customers, or both.

Relationships are the dynamic result of interactions between people and groups. They are fluid, always changing. They typically involve many types and levels of communication. And they are based on some type of commonality—for example, a common goal (working together); "common" time or space (that is, they share the experience of being together in some way); or common interests. Some relationships are chosen by us (friendships); others happen *to* us (coworkers, parents). The reality is, whatever the form the relationship takes, we all need them to truly flourish.

OUR INDIVIDUAL PERSPECTIVES

This book is the result of a team effort. And we believe much of its value comes from the unique perspective each of us as authors brings to the project.

Dr. Gary Chapman is best known for his #1 *New York Times* bestseller *The 5 Love Languages*. He has written numerous books on marriage, parenting, forgiveness, friendships, unique challenges in families, and workplace relationships. Trained as a marriage therapist and pastor, his expertise lies in how to develop and maintain healthy relationships.

Dr. Jennifer Thomas is a business consultant and psychologist. Jennifer developed the concept of apology languages and has given a TEDx talk on the subject. She and Dr. Chapman co-authored *The 5 Apology Languages*, applying research they conducted for the book.

Dr. Paul White is a psychologist whose focus has been to "make work relationships work." While working with successful family-owned businesses and dealing with the family issues intertwined with business succession planning, he saw the opportunity to apply the five love languages to work-based relationships. He and Dr. Chapman have co-authored three books: *The 5 Languages of Appreciation in the Workplace, Sync or Swim* (a fable about working together as a team), and *Rising Above a Toxic Workplace*. He is also the author of *The Vibrant Workplace*.

SUCCESS—THROUGH CHALLENGES

While we affirm the reality that conflicts, arguments, and friction will always be a part of working together with others, this is neither discouraging nor disconcerting to us. Healthy relationships occur *along with* clashes and disputes, even in the workplace! We know this to be true because we've seen (and been involved in) workplaces where people struggle to get along but still work together well. For example, I (Paul) worked in a counseling center where one of my colleagues and I had difficulties connecting and collaborating together for quite a while. We were different in many ways—our cultural backgrounds, our worldviews, our personalities, and how we approached tasks. Initially we struggled to communicate, often misunderstanding one another. This pattern, as you can imagine, led to frequent tension. However, we remained committed to working on our relationship and each strove to understand the other more fully. Over time, we developed a deep friendship rooted in mutual respect for one another.

Researchers also have repeatedly documented that healthy workplaces (and successful businesses) *do* experience conflict and have learned to manage friction. In fact, some research has shown the benefits of embracing differences of perspective in helping team members come up with more effective solutions to problems.

If companies are going to succeed, their teams must be working in unison. Each employee is a person of value who should be treated with respect. Thriving companies have a foundational recognition that people matter. Our book will help companies live out their values by learning how to handle conflict in positive ways. This includes:

- understanding the various underlying issues that create conflict
- mastering simple actions to help you avoid unnecessary relational difficulties
- discerning the most appropriate steps to resolve disagreements
- preventing toxic attitudes and interactions from taking root

- learning how, why, and when to apologize
- discovering the pathway to letting go of past hurts
- applying the steps needed to build (and rebuild) trust in a relationship.

We are excited about the journey you are about to start—traveling down the pathway of developing and repairing healthy workplace relationships in the midst of the normal misunderstandings and disagreements that happen when people work together.

Visit 5lovelanguages.com to take the *Making Things Right at Work* Apology Assessment online.

For Group Discussion

---

1. *Can you remember, in a prior work situation, someone with whom you struggled to get along? Why do you think you had difficulties in your relationship? Were you able to improve the quality of the relationship over time? If so, how?*

2. *Have you ever worked in a setting where everyone got along, and there was no conflict at all? If so, do you think everyone actually liked one another, or was the apparent "peace" due to an avoidance of conflict or desire not to hurt anyone's feelings?*

3. *How realistic do you believe it is to expect a lack of conflict at work? Is there an acceptable level of conflict or tension for you?*

COMMON CAUSES OF CONFLICT AT WORK

CHAPTER 1

WHY CONFLICT HAPPENS

BUT WHY CONFLICT? Where does it come from? Let's zero in on actual people and offenses. Like any good problem solving, specifying what the actual "problem" is and where it is coming from is the first step. So what about our example in the Introduction— the employee (we'll call her Kaylie) who felt demeaned when her boss (we'll call her Lori) seemed to dismiss and almost laugh at her idea in the meeting?

Kaylie needs to remember that the *symptoms* (Lori being dismissive) are not necessarily the *problem*. When you have an aching back, you can take some painkillers. But until you address the issue causing the pain, the symptom will probably return. So the first question to try to answer is *why* is Lori relating to Kaylie differently? Putting it another way, why is Kaylie feeling hurt by her boss, with whom she has gotten along well and who has always given her stellar reviews?

ALL OR NOTHING?

In general, Kaylie and Lori enjoy a solid working relationship. They don't socialize after hours or even have lunch together except for work functions. Lori is married with kids, a few years older than single Kaylie. But they get along. Then there's Sam, another of Lori's direct reports. He's hard for Kaylie to like—overly chatty and jokey. But he gets his work done and is never offensive or inappropriate, so she tolerates his dad jokes.

We need to remind ourselves that having problems with someone is not an "all or nothing" experience. It's not a choice of cherished confidant or nameless stranger. The quality and level of our relationships exists on a continuum, as do the challenges in those relationships. Some people may irritate us a little bit. Others we really enjoy—but only up to a point, and then we need a break from them.

We seem to be able to communicate clearly and easily with some people at work, while there are others who we don't "get," and they don't get us. Coming to the point where we understand one another takes a lot of time and effort (and sometimes doesn't seem worth it!).

Within the context of work relationships, we may have a colleague who becomes a close friend we enjoy spending time with outside of work. We probably have coworkers we're not close to, but we work together well. Sometimes a colleague (or a supervisor or someone we supervise) rubs us the wrong way because of our significant differences in personality and communication styles. And then there are those we either actively dislike or have a past conflict that continues to cloud our relationship.

Finally (and hopefully they are rare), there may be people in the organization you don't feel safe around, or with whom you have serious differences about important things. You might choose to minimize your contact with them. If at all possible, *these people should not be in a direct reporting relationship with you.* If this is the case, work to make changes until you can honestly say that you have a positive relationship with all of your supervisors and supervisees.

TEMPORARY "BREAKS"

But even the most positive workplace relationships can be fractured by a temporary "break" in the relationship—maybe not a complete break where you don't relate at all, but clearly tension, mistrust, or hurt has come between you two. What causes such fractures?

Misunderstanding / Miscommunication

Probably the most common source of challenges in workplace interactions comes from simple misunderstanding and miscommunication. Mishearing (literally, not accurately hearing what the other person said) and misinterpreting the message they intended to send are the reason so much training in communication and "active listening" is foundational to workplace functioning. One of the best ways to avoid this type of miscommunication is to confirm that you understand the message sent and the practical implications (that is, what is expected of you in response). Simply summarizing what you've heard ("What I hear you saying is . . . and you want me to . . . ") is an excellent tool to use consistently when communicating with your coworkers and superiors. It could be Kaylie, for whatever reason, misheard or certainly misinterpreted Lori—or the other way around.

Differing Viewpoints / Perspectives / Opinions / Preferences

Some conflicts are the result of honest differences with others. These are normal, and in many cases healthy, providing a variety of viewpoints and reflecting the wide range of backgrounds and values in our culture and the growing diversity of our workforce. Real-life examples include:

- One of your team members disagrees with you regarding the direction the marketing plan should go.
- You disagree with some of your coworkers on the role of government in helping people.
- Your boss comes from an older generation. His preferences for the colors, fonts, and images that he wants to use in branding the company vary widely from your and your colleagues' ideas.

Dissimilar Personality and Communication Styles

Relational challenges frequently derive from distinct personality styles and their associated communication patterns. A myriad of personality typologies have been developed that describe people's personality traits in a variety of categories. These approaches can focus on interpersonal energy (introversion/extroversion); inner motivations that drive behaviors (the Kolbe Index, the Enneagram); ways of perceiving the world around them (the Myers Briggs Type Indicator); how they approach tasks (the DISC); and many other ways of assessing personality traits.[1]

Think about the problems that can ensue when you have two department heads working together on a project. One has a strong, forceful, in-your-face style, while the other is more soft-spoken, waits to talk until there is "space" open in the conversation, and tends to avoid confrontational interactions. Without significant help—say, from a third person in the mix—they may have trouble making decisions and accomplishing tasks, simply because of who they are and what their communication styles are.

We need a diverse array of personality types in a work setting to avoid the dangers of "groupthink." At the same time, continually wrestling through these differences can be stressful and draining. We perceive events differently, bring divergent values to bear on a situation, react differently to challenges, and communicate our views and beliefs in distinctive ways. This is why most of us prefer to be around others seemingly "like us"—it's just easier. The downside is that, when everyone has a shared viewpoint, we can collectively make wrong decisions without the "team of rivals" effect of varied opinions and backgrounds.

Unintentional Mistakes

We all make mistakes. We forget to complete a task. We don't remember to include all relevant team members on an important email. We accidentally hit "reply all" and copy too many team members on an email that contains negative information about an employee. Some of us share our thoughts and opinions before fully thinking them through. We write down the wrong date for a meeting or a deadline. We're too hasty in reviewing the numbers on a financial report. We may draw an erroneous conclusion from information we've heard before fully checking out the actual facts (and context) of a situation. The potential examples are almost as numerous as the number of decisions made in daily work life.

There are also *intentional* errors—we discuss those below.

The problem is, most of the time when an employee makes a mistake (regardless of intent), someone else is affected negatively. The error provides inaccurate information from which a decision is made. The miscommunication may create a false perception of a person, company, or product. Just as good decisions are built upon accurate information, poor decisions are often the consequence of inaccurate data and perceptions. And poor decisions may affect the health of the organization, your vendors, your customers, and the community at large.

Who is to blame when unintentional mistakes occur? No one, really. Mistakes happen, and playing the blame game doesn't help. What does? Identifying how the mistake happened, piecing together who (or what process) is responsible for some parts of the error occurring. This leads to determining what corrective steps need to be taken toward those affected, and provides direction on what steps can be taken to try to prevent a similar mistake happening in the future.

Feeling Offended or Disrespected

When you (or someone in your organization) feels offended or disrespected by someone, we would argue that assuming that the "offending" party did something wrong is not the best place to start. Why? Because sometimes people become offended when nothing improper was actually done.

Our response of feeling offended or disrespected comes from the experience of not feeling treated appropriately by someone. They either did something we think they "shouldn't have" (refer to the boss as "Jim" versus "Mr. Atkins"), or they *didn't* do something we think they should have (copy you on an email regarding an issue that affects you and the department you oversee). Or, as we saw earlier, feeling put down in some way, as happened with Kaylie and her boss.

Since each of us carries around myriad unspoken expectations, often shaped by deep-rooted values, innumerable opportunities to offend or feel offended arise every day, especially in new situations where the workplace culture and social norms are still developing. This also happens when teammates from different cultures are interacting.

From our work with the five languages of appreciation in the workplace, we have learned that people are also more sensitive to various modes of communication based on their preferred appreciation language. For example, a colleague who values *Quality Time* may feel hurt when they are not invited to go to lunch with the rest of the team. Or a coworker for whom *Words of Affirmation* are important may be more sensitive to verbal correction than generally would be expected.

WRONG CHOICES AND INAPPROPRIATE ACTIONS

A final category of actions needs to be discussed—when someone (you, your colleague, a supervisor) actually makes a poor choice. The action or reaction displayed clearly falls below the commonly accepted standard of what is appropriate for that situation. Usually the "appropriateness" of the action is defined by relevant societal norms or according to the organizational culture, but can also be influenced by an individual's cultural background, their personal experiences, and their own values and priorities.

The range of behaviors that are viewed as inappropriate are almost limitless, but let us share a few common examples we have observed and/or experienced (or done ourselves):

- A leader "calling out" a team member in front of others for not getting a task done on time or at the expected quality level, using an intense tone of voice and derogatory language ("I can't believe you were so stupid to believe that is what we wanted for this presentation.").
- Not understanding the expectations for the type of clothing to wear to an event and creating embarrassment for your boss, organization, and yourself. This can take the form of either being noticeably underdressed—

wearing shorts, t-shirt, and sandals to a more formal
event where slacks, a collared shirt, and leather shoes
are expected. Or misunderstanding what "formal attire"
means in your company's (or industry's) culture—a
coat and tie are expected for men and a nice dress or
business suit for women, not a tuxedo or a full-length,
high-society formal gown.

- When a presentation doesn't go well, lying to your
supervisor about your role and responsibility, placing
blame on a colleague.

These actions, in different ways, cross boundaries of what is permissible and understandable. To a degree, "what's permissible" may
vary according to your own company's culture or industry norms.
Dressing inappropriately may be a minor gaffe, easily remedied, in
one organization; in another, it may be viewed as a major faux pas.
On the other hand, throwing a teammate under the bus, or public
shaming of someone, could have very serious repercussions—for
you, not them.

Whatever the infraction, whatever the line that is crossed, you
will need to make things right and perhaps repair a relationship.
Later in this book we will look at the role apologies may play in
the workplace.

For Group Discussion

1. *When you think about the various sources of
relational conflict you have experienced at work,
which of these is the most common for you?*

- *misunderstanding/miscommunication*
- *differing viewpoints and perspectives*
- *dissimilar personalities and communication styles*
- *unintentional mistakes and errors*
- *feeling offended or disrespected*

2. *Which of the sources of relational conflict (above) do you see displayed most frequently by others in your workplace?*

CHAPTER 2

THE FIVE LANGUAGES OF BEING OFFENDED

HAVE YOU EVER NOTICED that some people seem rather "touchy"—that it doesn't take much to upset them? Or how about those times when a usually calm colleague turns prickly in their interactions with you?

Obviously, a person's tendency to be more irritable than usual has many sources—physical pain, emotional stress, lack of sleep, worries weighing on them—the list is almost endless.

But in talking with employees and supervisors, an important theme emerged that might not be obvious. Many people report that they become more irritable and offended when they don't feel valued or appreciated for their contributions. They say they haven't heard anything positive about the work they are doing or acknowledgment for successfully overseeing a completed project.

This issue should be taken seriously because research has shown that 79 percent of employees who leave a job voluntarily cite a lack of appreciation as one of the key contributing factors to their deciding to quit.[1]

We have learned that a person's preferred ways of receiving appreciation (what we call their "Primary Language of Appreciation") is also the language through which they tend to be most easily *offended*. Think of it this way: the issue is similar to people having various preferences about the type of technology they like to use to communicate with others—talking on the phone, texting, video, chatting, email, even possibly talking in person! And they use their preferred medium of communication to both *send* and *receive* information.

Similarly, we have found that a person's preferred language of appreciation is the medium of communication to which they are most sensitive. For a colleague who values Quality Time, individual time with them communicates appreciation to them more effectively than giving them a verbal compliment. Helping a team member who is working on a time-sensitive project will be more encouraging to them if their primary language is Acts of Service, rather than giving them a small gift (like their favorite dessert).

So the appreciation languages work both ways. Using the languages, and the actions within that language that are important to them,[2] will help others "hit the mark" when trying to communicate appreciation or encouragement. But, as we will present below, their primary language of appreciation also is frequently the means of communication (or lack of it) by which they are most easily *offended*. For example, if you have a colleague or supervisor who seems to get upset when given even a little corrective verbal feedback, a strong likelihood exists that their primary language of appreciation is Words of Affirmation. Let's examine the five languages of appreciation in the workplace[3] and see how this principle applies to each.

WORDS OF AFFIRMATION

We know that for about 45 percent to 50 percent of the workforce, words are very important.[4] And in the workplace, we most commonly show appreciation and gratitude for our colleagues through words. We express praise, we give compliments, and we tell people "thanks." People like compliments, but they want your words to be specific. "Thanks for staying late to help me finish up inventory." "I appreciate how you've adjusted to remote working." A text that says, "Hey, thanks for having my back in the meeting this morning." A generic "Good job!" doesn't cut it.

Those who value words seem to be sensitive to perceived negative comments. You think you're doling out constructive criticism. They hear "You're not doing very well," and get sad or defensive. The feedback contains valuable insight on areas where they need to learn and grow, but maybe they take it harder than we intended. Be gentler with corrective feedback with these people; it doesn't take much to get their attention.

One woman we know said, "I cannot stand 'constructive criticism.' Often I KNOW all too well what I need to do better. The best bosses I've ever had understand that about me. Tell me good things I'm doing and deliver the 'how you can improve' message with a heaping dose of encouragement."

These folks can also be offended by what they perceive as caustic or critical comments. If you're the kind of person to toss off a sarcastic jab but say, "Oh, I was just joking," know that not everyone shares your sense of humor. Be careful about flippant remarks in their presence.

QUALITY TIME

Not all quality time is the same. Yes, for some folks time spent with those they care about is more meaningful and encouraging than anything else. But the specifics differ with each individual. Some people may want an unhurried one-on-one with their supervisor—not involving performance evaluation. Others might prefer happy hour with their peers. Still others enjoy the stimulation of a "lunch and learn" with different departments, while others might relish a catch-up Zoom call with a favorite teammate.

Younger employees highly value peer relationships. Overall, people choose quality time as their preferred way to be appreciated more than 25 percent of the time; hence, one in four of your team members values this language.

Those whose appreciation language is quality time can be offended in three primary ways:

For supervisors: Scheduling a meeting with the employee and repeatedly rescheduling, canceling, or totally blowing off and forgetting the meeting. This clearly communicates that other things are more important to you than they are.

For colleagues: Leaving them out (either intentionally or unintentionally—the result is the same) when you go out to lunch or invite a group of people for a social event. This includes quiet coworkers—even introverts like to be invited and participate in social gatherings with a small group of friends. Even if you're pretty sure they'll say no, *people like to be asked.*

For anyone: For the people who value quality time above all, focused attention is paramount. Eye contact. Listening. Engaging. And so if you are with them, block out your distractions. Because if you're doing something else—answering the phone, glancing at your texts and sending even quick replies, letting yourself be interrupted by another colleague, checking the TV in the restaurant to see how the game is coming—you have essentially told them, "Hey, I'm not really here with you. You're not that important."

And so you really need to make sure when you are spending time with those who highly value quality time that you keep your appointments. Second, include them in small group gatherings. And third, get any distractions out of the way so they have your total, focused attention.

ACTS OF SERVICE

Acts of service is an important appreciation language for a lot of people—and is highly relevant in work settings. In fact, more than one of every five employees (21 percent) chooses this as their primary language of appreciation. One of the things that we've learned is that for people who strongly value acts of service, these expressions are *really important* to them. You may remember sayings like "Talk is cheap" or "Don't tell me you care—show me." That's how these people think, and if you don't do something actively to show that they're of value and you want to support them, it doesn't matter how much you say or what kind of words you use, you're going to miss the mark. For example, stopping by their workstation at 5:30 p.m. as they're staring at their screen, desk cluttered with papers, trying to get the financials completed in time for tomorrow's executive board meeting. You say, "Wow, way to go. Hope you get that project done. Well, we're taking off—game starts early. Hey, if you get finished, come down and join us. Go Jayhawks!" And off you and your happy crew go.

Such "encouragement" will not land well with an acts of service person. They will probably mumble some response—but inwardly they will be fuming. What they want to hear from you is:

"Wow, you're here late. Need a hand?" They may not always take you up on it, but they want to hear it.

Now, for some people for whom acts of service is important, it's less about getting the task done and more about doing it *with people*. They like the camaraderie of working on something together. One woman we know who fits this profile said, "I remember in one office I worked at years ago, I had to step in and help with a big mailing. Really boring. But I remember this one admin, while we were working together, told stories about growing up in the sandhill country of Nebraska—in a literal sod house, in the Depression. So the time went fast!" Keep an eye out for simple tasks you can do with others.

But one of the things you *don't* want to do is correct them or tell them how to do it better. Most of these people have thought through what they're doing and they have a process that works for them. It may not be the process that works for you, but this is not the time to give them advice. Stifle any urge to say, "Hey, have you thought about doing it this way?"—especially if you're just standing back and watching them work. Instead, ask them if they'd like some help. And often people say no initially, so watch for a bit. If you can see that they in fact do need help, say, "I've got some time—I'd really be glad to give you a hand." That brief act of service can grow a sense of support and loyalty, both from you and from them.

TANGIBLE GIFTS

First, a word of clarification. For those of you who are familiar with our definition of this concept, tangible gifts do *not* mean bonuses, rewards, or increased compensation. (Those are issues determined by the employer/employee contract.) A tangible gift as an act of appreciation or encouragement is a little token that shows you thought about the individual as a person, not just a name on the payroll or a line item on the budget. The gift need not be costly. The meaning comes in the personal touch. A perfect example would be if a boss gave the five people in her department gift cards for Christmas—and each of the cards reflected a different interest (dogs, gourmet cooking, running . . . so many possibilities).

Interestingly, people who value gifts aren't necessarily upset if they *don't* receive something (although they may if they never get anything over a long period of time). What does offend them is when everyone gets the same thing for a holiday—like a mug filled with candy canes. They are not going to refuse the gift, but they're going to realize the giver didn't really spend a lot of time thinking about the item or, more to the point, the person. It is the personal nature of the gift that is meaningful to them.

PHYSICAL TOUCH

Touch? In the workplace? Yes. Many individuals' first response is: "Physical touch! That's not allowed at work. You are just asking to be sued!" Clearly, while appropriate physical touch is a normal part of life in many relationships, we know that physical touch in the workplace can be problematic. Actions that are acceptable for some people make others uncomfortable. Also, some regions of the US, and certain ethnic cultures, are much more at ease with physical touch than others. (Obviously, we exclude any type of touch that is perceived as sexual or intrusive.) Why, then, even talk about physical touch in the workplace? Because *appropriate* physical touch continues to be a part of many workplace relationships, largely in the form of *spontaneous celebration*.

Celebrating among colleagues is the most common reason for an act of "connecting" physically at work. Touch can be a means of expressing excitement and joy. A high five for completing a major project, a fist-bump for solving a problem, a congratulatory handshake for closing a large sale, or a pat on the back when a colleague receives an award—all are examples of celebrating together through physical touch.

But . . . even these expressions of joy and appreciation can be offensive when used inappropriately, or when the action makes a colleague uncomfortable.

Our research has shown that physical touch is rarely anyone's primary appreciation language in the majority culture in the US or Canada. However, that is not the case in other cultures or even in some other minority ethnic cultures in the US. Clearly, our Latin American friends and Hispanics value touch, as do other Southern European societies (Italians, for example). In many other cultures outside of North America, touch is very important. So we don't want to overreact against touch and even run the risk of offending valued colleagues or customers.

The easiest way to offend somebody is to touch them when they don't want to be touched at all—or they don't want to be touched by you. You have to remember that it's not just the action of touch, but who's doing the touching. But on the other side of things, among people for whom touch is important, you might unwittingly offend them by acting cool and defensive, treating them like they're "weird," especially if you attribute negative intent to what they see as a gesture of warmth.

There are many for whom physical touch is not their primary language, but they enjoy the connection of a high five or fist bump, pat on the back, or even a quick side hug. They too might be offended if you react negatively to their kind gesture. Say instead, "Hey, I'm not a hugger, but I can do a high five."

It is beyond the scope of this book to explore truly inappropriate, threatening, or triggering touch in a professional situation, or even expressions of affection between "work friends" that breach the boundaries of such relationships. There are many resources available that unpack these issues. And you and your team may decide that, given the complexities around these questions, your approach will be "if in doubt, don't." These things are deeply personal. But we trust this discussion of physical touch in the workplace can be a helpful starting point.

POSITIVE AND NEGATIVE

It seems reasonable that the channel of communication which has the most impact on an individual *positively* would also be the medium through which they are most sensitive to *negative* messages (either real or perceived).

Understanding the relationship between individuals' languages of appreciation and tendency to feel offended by actions (or inaction) in that language can give you some insight into why they seem to be irritable and defensive when no other reason is evident. You may want to check out what their primary language of appreciation is[5]—it may give you clues on underlying relational dynamics.

We hope these insights will help you understand why some of your coworkers may be reacting coolly toward you—and why you, in turn, might have problems with them.

For Group Discussion

1. As you read about these languages of appreciation and "being offended," does one of them
ring more true for you? How about people you
work with?

2. Do you think physical touch has any place in a
work setting, or not? Does your company have a
well-developed corporate policy around these
issues?

3. Regarding communication and cultural differences in the workplace, have you experienced
challenges where someone was offended due
to cultural differences? How did you handle the
situation?

STRATEGIES FOR AVOIDING UNNECESSARY CONFLICT

CHAPTER 3

WHERE IT STARTS: EFFECTIVE COMMUNICATION

HECTOR'S HOUSE WAS DARK. His wife and children were sleeping peacefully. Hector should have been in bed on this work night. But he was up, on his laptop, feverishly trying to finish an assessment of a proposal his boss had asked for. It was due in the morning . . . only a few hours off. Hector was fairly new in the company and wanted to make a good impression. So, fueled by coffee and adrenaline, he sat at his kitchen island, tapping away. There! He proofread the document, and emailed it to his boss.

Driving in to work, he got a text on his screen: "Come by when you get in." *What?*

He had commented on the wrong proposal.

As we've already seen, bad things can happen when an employee misunderstands or mishears what a teammate or boss is saying. Not all conflicts in the workplace are the result of major events that cause serious relational breaks between coworkers. In fact, we believe that most relational difficulties in the workplace stem from minor "glitches" that can be addressed through a variety of relational and work-based strategies.

We posit that using these healthy communication processes will allow you to *avoid* many disagreements and conflicts that, like weeds in a garden, are just waiting to sprout and grow if not attended to. These tools are at the heart of much of the leadership training that goes on in organizations and companies across the globe.

Clearly, learning about and implementing these processes can significantly reduce the need to go through the more intense process of correcting breaks in relationships between colleagues, employees and supervisors, with vendors and customers. The ancient saying, "An ounce of prevention is better than a pound of cure" applies here.

Let's begin by giving you some tools to reduce the amount of conflict you have to manage at work, and also strategies to help keep the intensity of the disagreements low so they can be resolved more easily. We've identified five key sets of skills that can improve your relationships at work—and that you can teach to your team members so everyone gets along better! Topics in this section will include:

1. Checking for understanding with active listening
2. Clarifying misperceptions, misinterpretations, and misattributions of motives
3. Committing to direct (versus indirect) communication
4. Avoiding the various forms of deception
5. Accepting that others view the world differently than you (and that's okay)

We guarantee that if you work on building these behaviors into your daily interactions, you will see the number and intensity of disagreements at work decline significantly.

CAN YOU HEAR ME?
THE BENEFITS OF ACTIVE LISTENING

With our busy lives, misunderstandings are inevitable. You can prevent many conflicts by simply slowing down, setting aside distractions, and offering your full attention to the person who is speaking. What gets in the way of doing this? Multitasking. We're in the habit of completing emails, responding to texts, and doing online shopping while trying to listen with one ear. You might reason that you're making efficient use of your time, but too often it becomes a bad habit. Do this today—consciously set aside your phone and remove other distractions when people are talking to you. Give them both of your ears and both of your eyes. On top of that, don't rush them along by completing their sentences. Offer them the gift of your unhurried time. Listen completely.

WHAT DOES RUSHED, REJECTING,
OR INVALIDATING COMMUNICATION
LOOK LIKE IN DAILY LIFE?

Too often, our thoughts and feelings are met with criticism. Here are some examples of invalidating phrases I (Paul) have heard in companies:

- Okay, okay, I get the picture. Let's move on.
- You *really* think that?
- Where did you come up with a crazy idea like that?

- That would never work. We need to do this instead.
- I keep telling you, that's a really bad idea. Forget about it.
- We don't have the budget to do what you're suggesting.
- That has already been tried. It failed, so we're not going to try again.

Poor listening exacts a high price in the long run. And a negative, distracted, or hurried response can have serious consequences:

- Employees may feel extremely hurt by criticism of their ideas.
- Feelings of anger are stirred up.
- Employees become dissatisfied and quit working— whether or not they leave the company.
- Beneficial creativity shuts down.
- Healthy brainstorming ceases.
- Growth slows to a snail's pace.

WHAT TO DO AFTER OTHERS SPEAK? SHOW YOUR UNDERSTANDING

Maybe you, as a colleague or manager, have been guilty of a hurried response, or sounding negative when you didn't intend to be, or, like Hector, missing the assignment entirely. Listening carefully only gets you part of the way. You could just glibly say, "Got it! Let's go." But you shouldn't do that. The next, critical step is to *check with the other person for understanding.* Summarize what they said and what, if anything, they want you to do. The other person will usually tell you whether or not you got it right, but be sure to ask if it's needed. If they make adjustments or corrections, you should repeat the process of summarizing what they said and include their clarification. Ask again whether your summary covered all of the bases. Pro tip: Try to add an image when you summarize their message. It feels great when someone else listens carefully enough to put a picture around your own situation or feelings.

But what if you completely disagree with what the other person is saying? Conventional wisdom says to listen only long enough to form a good counter-argument in your head. But this is very short-sighted. If you are going to disagree with someone else, it's far more useful to repeat their arguments first. This heads off one big question in their mind when you attempt to make your own case: that you simply misunderstood what they were trying to say. In addition, it shows your respect for the other person despite your differences. We can validate the views of others even when we don't hold the same position. The practice of restating the arguments of others, *especially* when you think they are wrong, requires maturity and practice. This skill can be learned through patience and practice.

HOW TO CREATE HARMONY AT WORK

As consultants, we've spent a great deal of time with unhappy pairs. Some are couples. Others are work partners. A few are both at once! They usually arrive with many stories to tell about how their partner has upset and disappointed them. Rather than having them repeat their list of complaints, I (Gary) try to switch things up. Often, I ask them to tell me what their partner is concerned about. It's interesting to watch how long they can talk about the other person without launching into their own version of events.

What is the most essential tool for harmony at work? It all begins with listening.

DO:

- Be respectful.
- Learn their appreciation language and speak it instead of your own.
- Convey gratitude.
- Show interest in their ideas.
- Repeat what they have said to show that you understand them even if you disagree.
- Note: If people are repeating themselves, it may be a sign that they don't think everyone really "got it." They won't stop repeating themselves until you show that you understand them. Contradicting them won't work. Earn their attention by showing you have noted their points.
- Smile and laugh. Glowering makes problems seem bigger. Smiling makes life more fun.

DON'T do these things because they are hostile, spark defensiveness, and shut down communication:

- Point your finger.
- Yell.
- Slam or throw things.
- Cuss or call names.
- Cross your arms defensively.
- Use extreme words like "always," "none," and "never." This is rarely true and it invites squabbling.
- Blame others or make excuses for yourself.
- Deny problems you have caused.
- Mock and mimic.

Additionally, do not escalate an argument in front of your team, draw your coworkers into the fray, or refuse to let the other person leave when they have asked for some breathing room.

For Group Discussion

1. *One of the reasons we sometimes fail to confirm what the other person said is because we don't want to "look stupid" in front of our workmate or certainly the boss. So we say "Sure! Got it!" when inwardly we aren't sure. Are you hesitant to ask for clarification? Has this ever proved a mistake?*

2. *Excuse-making is rampant in our society and often in our workplaces. How do you handle it when an employee or colleague habitually makes excuses for not delivering on a task?*

CHAPTER 4

THE DANGER OF MAKING ASSUMPTIONS

THIS IS A STORY ABOUT assuming the worst of someone.

George and Emily both work for a national health care company. When Emily was given an additional area to supervise (telehealth), she asked for help from a regional manager in her company named George who had specialized training in her new area.

What happened next? George gave Emily all the advice she wanted—and more. He had developed a reputation for being controlling and overreaching. Emily soon understood why. She already had one boss, Arlene, and she didn't want another one in the person of George.

It has been said that employees don't quit their job; they quit their boss. I (Jennifer) would add that employees also quit their coworkers.

By the time Emily came to me for consultation, she was ready to leave her job, and she had already posted her résumé online.

In Emily's company, there was a clear chain of command, but George, in the name of being helpful, was injecting himself into too many situations. Emily was exasperated by George "acting like he was my new manager and questioning so many things I was doing." She resented him and felt like he was trying to tell her how to do her job and maybe even become her boss.

For his part, George was blindsided by the pushback he received from Emily and others. He had no intention of becoming her boss. He just wanted to help Emily, and therefore the organization. But when your desire is to help, criticism can feel devaluing and devastating.

What could Emily do? My first job was to fill Emily in on the problem of *misattributions*.

THE STORIES THAT HURT RELATIONSHIPS

Negative attributions—that is, negative assumptions about others—are one of the greatest unrecognized threats to relationship breakdowns and a primary cause of employees feeling unappreciated at work. Author Brené Brown calls attributions "the stories we tell ourselves in our heads." We'll demystify these automatic stories that lead to catastrophic relationship breakdowns. How can we nail down something so amorphous as a lack of trust? By looking at attributions that are spoken. Attributions are the motives we assign to others.[1]

Your brain has a wonderful way of making split-second judgments about time, distance, and safety. Most of these judgments are right on target—but not all. Assuming the worst of another person (without any evidence) will bring you nothing but trouble. When you misjudge others, you destroy relationships. When someone mislabels your motives, your trust is gone before they even finish their accusation. Put another way, your trust is drained by *any false assumptions* of negative motives. If the "story" I tell myself in my head is that you don't trust me to work without being microman-aged, then I'm shooting holes in our work relationship. No matter how often you try to speak my primary language of appreciation, I'll dismiss your efforts. Attributions are unconscious. But you can learn to spot them by watching for these red flags:

- First, assuming that others dislike you, think you're not valuable, or don't care about your needs. For example, saying, "You only wrote me an encouraging note be-cause someone else told you to." When you react with mistrust because of your own hidden beliefs, you break the other person's trust.
- Second, assuming the worst in others. For example, thinking, "You secretly want to get rid of me." When you lash out at them because you sense danger, they wonder why your trust evaporated and the forest fire of misunderstanding grows. When the smoke clears, some relationships have been broken beyond repair.

What happened in Emily's work situation? She scheduled a Zoom session with George in which she sandwiched her limits (or boundaries) between two positive messages for George. Emily said this to George:

"George, you have been generous with your time in helping me get up to speed on telehealth practice. I'd like to circle back to something I did that was unclear. I asked you for help without tell-ing you when I would be ready to take the ball back. I appreciate your help, and I'm ready to run on my own now. If I need your help down the road, I'll call you. Thank you very much for your help."

When we are working within stressful circumstances or a

tense working relationship, we are especially at risk of misreading others' motives. What may usually be a normal comment or question ("When do you think you will have that report done?") can take on negative connotations when communicated within a tense environment. We may think, "Do they think I'm not competent to do my job? I get my work done on time!" or "She's just trying to make me look bad in front of my supervisor by asking that question in front of them!"

Misattributing negative motives to a colleague is especially likely to occur when we have had past conflicts with them (and the issue is still unresolved). If we are hurt or angry from past interactions, we're at risk for assuming the person desires to make us "look bad" to others or to hurt our career.

We have found that many times our own motivations for our actions are difficult to discern, and that determining the internal thoughts, feelings, and motives of others is virtually impossible to accurately perceive without communicating with them directly. As a result, we have concluded that, almost always, the best course of action to take is to give others the benefit of the doubt when attributing motives to others' actions or statements.

Misperceiving Intent

Misattributions are all around us, but they can be subtle and rather hard to put our finger on. Here is an example: Mary kicked off the story of her day with this blunt complaint: "My coworker teased me, and she really hurt my feelings. I thought I was trying to do something good and she twisted it, making it sound like my motives were bad."

She went on to explain her situation. "You see, I'm a hesitant blood donor. It had always made me feel sick. But I think it's important, so I occasionally do it against my own judgment. I always

try to get a friend to go with me—both for moral support and because misery loves company. I announced to my whole office that
I really wanted to donate blood one week. I asked whether anyone
would be willing to go and donate blood alongside me—especially
since the agency would be including a free COVID antibody test.

"Guess how my teasing coworker responded? 'Mary, you're
just donating blood so you can get tested for COVID, aren't you?'"

Mary continued, "I should have said 'Ouch!' Her words hit
me like a slap on the face, especially because I am such a reluctant blood donor. But I defended myself, agreeing that I was using
COVID as a selling point for encouraging others to go, *but* that
it wasn't the only or even the main reason I was going to donate
blood. I wouldn't say it was great interaction, but we were able
to move on from it. I donated blood alone, and the topic hasn't
come up again."

Misperceiving Motives

In a relatively new company that was growing steadily, Megan,
the Chief Operating Officer, was trying to formalize some processes so that, as the company grew, these procedures would grow
in place as standard practices.

One process that she was trying to implement was for the team
members who reported directly to her to "cc" her on important
emails they sent to significant clients and suppliers—both to keep
her in the loop but also to provide documentation for the future.

Talia, who managed relationships with some key clients, resented the request, feeling like Megan didn't trust her to handle
the relationships well. (Additionally, Talia's preferred mode of
communication was to give verbal reports rather than by email.)
She felt that Megan was micromanaging her.

Over a series of months, they had several discussions about

the requested procedure. Megan was frustrated that Talia repeatedly didn't comply with Megan's request—to the point that it became part of Talia's behavior goals and performance reviews. Talia continued to view the issue as primarily a lack of trust in her abilities, as well as a bit of a control issue for Megan. As a result, she continued to be defensive and would only comply with the process occasionally.

Ultimately, a business coach, who was working with both Megan and Talia individually, discussed the issue with Talia and challenged her misperceptions of Megan's motives. The coach affirmed to Talia that formalizing communication about client and supplier relationships through email *and* to include one's supervisor in the communication was not only a common business practice, but that it was a healthy one when developing processes as more team members came on board.

With this encouragement, Talia started copying Megan on significant emails (which Megan positively affirmed her for), and the procedure became a non-issue over time.

Misperceiving Value

One of the most common areas of tension in business is the issue of financial compensation for employees. Team members routinely get bent out of shape when they discover (often accidentally) how much more money a colleague is earning than they are. Common responses include: "They're not worth that much!" "Don't they see how much value I bring to the organization?"

The challenge is: an individual's value to the company is not the only factor that influences the level of compensation. Other components include: a) the industry in which you work and the corresponding value *society* gives to the area (for example, professional sports vs. teachers); b) the level of technical skill and training for the position (speech therapist vs. surgeon); c) the demand for the position and scarcity of qualified people (cybersecurity specialists); and d) location (New York City vs. Hot Springs, Arkansas).

One more element should be mentioned: one's role within the company. Most employees can't comprehend why high-level salespersons earn so much money (sometimes more than the president or COO of the company.) In fact, I (Paul) have had to grow in my understanding of this issue over the years. I grew up in the context of a family-owned business, and I remember intense discussions among the family members about how much money John (our top salesperson) made. But the fact of the matter was that John had a good working relationship with the buyers of our major client. And because this one company accounted for over one-third of our company's sales, John's value to the company was huge—without the sales he brought in, our business wouldn't have been profitable and wouldn't have survived in the long run.

As I've consulted with family-owned businesses, the issue of value and the tension associated with it has been repeated numerous times. "How can [top salesman] be worth so much?" The answer is: because without sales, the company ceases to exist. You can have the best product, outstanding customer service, efficient processes, great communication and decision-making procedures. But if you don't have sufficient sales, "You ain't got nothin.'"

This issue played itself out within a small business when Janice, the office manager, inadvertently found out how much money Daniel, the sales manager, made (which included commissions based on the amount of sales he brought in.) Janice was a competent, dedicated team member who earned a salary commensurate with industry standards in her region of the country.

But when she found out by accident that Daniel (when including his commissions) made almost twice as much as she did, she was both hurt and livid. Holding back tears, she went to the company's president and exclaimed: "Don't you value what I do? I work hard and do everything you ask me to—and more! Daniel is a great guy and is good at his job, but I can't believe you think he is worth two times of what I contribute. If that is how you feel about me, I quit. I can't work in a place where I don't feel valued."

Even though the president attempted to listen to her concerns and help her understand the context, Janice was adamant and officially gave her two weeks' notice the following day.

Unfortunately, this is a classic example of a misperception of an individual's value with the financial compensation their position warrants.

For Group Discussion

1. *Why do you think we sometimes make "snap judgments" about people?*

2. *In a previous chapter we discussed reflecting back what we had heard someone communicate. Reflect on the connection between assuming and clarifying communication.*

CHAPTER 5

THE (HIGH) COST OF INDIRECT COMMUNICATION

IN THE PAST, WHEN I (PAUL) would conduct leadership training for organizations on the five languages of appreciation, frequently at breaks or after the training, people would come up to me and share their stories of how nasty their workplace was, or what a jerk their boss was.

This experience happened so often that I began to wonder how bad the workplace cultures were (and how many unhealthy ones there were). So I decided to ask for feedback from our newsletter subscribers—and I was overwhelmed with the hundreds of responses we received. We then followed up and interviewed a number of people to find out what was really going on in so many workplaces. The results of this investigation led to our book, *Rising Above a Toxic Workplace,* and a series of online training courses.[1]

One of the findings from our investigation was: *indirect communication is a key symptom of a toxic workplace.* When an organization is struggling to function effectively, you don't have to dig very deep to find lots of examples of indirect communication being used across the organization.

WHAT DOES INDIRECT COMMUNICATION LOOK LIKE IN WORK LIFE?

Unfortunately, indirect communication is not a singular, unitary problem. Communicating indirectly actually takes many forms *and* has a few different driving motivations. As a result, both factors lead to challenges in "stamping it out." Here are a number of common examples of the ways circuitous communication surfaces in workplace cultures:

- "Going around" the person you really should talk to.
- Talking about someone else (gossip) who is not directly involved in the problem or solution.
- Asking permission from the person you believe is most likely to say yes, even though they don't have direct authority to do so.
- Not saying what you really mean—"talking around" the issue, or possibly, hinting at the real message but not saying it forthrightly.
- Telling someone else to communicate a message for you (versus telling the ultimate recipient yourself).
- Giving a "softer" message than the actual content that needs to be communicated, hoping the recipient will read between the lines.
- Using nonverbal cues or tone of voice to communicate a different meaning than the words that are being communicated (raising of eyebrows, glances, sarcastic tone of voice).

WHY DO WE USE INDIRECT COMMUNICATION?

There are a variety of reasons we use indirect communication, depending on the outcome desired. Our motivations can include:

- Hoping to obtain a positive response to a request that probably wouldn't occur if the actual person who provides oversight were to be asked: *"Lisa, I can't find Noel anywhere. Is it okay if I go ahead and purchase these supplies? We really need them to get going on the Wilson project."*
- Reporting negative results straightforwardly, so the news won't sound as bad as it actually is: *"We didn't meet our projected profit goals last quarter, but we are looking forward to better results in the coming months"* (when there actually was a loss for the quarter).
- Trying to lay blame on someone else and/or undermine the perception of a colleague: *"You know Jenni said she didn't get the presentation completed because she was sick, but she actually went to visit her family all weekend."*
- Desiring to "hide" and not be associated with a negative action or result: *"Hey, Latisha, when you take those documents over to accounting, would you stop by Jeff's office and let him know we won't be getting payment from Smith & Co. for the work we did for them, for about six weeks or so?"*
- Attempting to avoid a negative reaction to the message being communicated: You send the following email to your supervisor after hours on Friday (when she was expecting the report to be completed and received): *"The report on the Hopkins case won't be ready until Monday."*

THE CONSEQUENCES

The choices we make between interacting directly with others, or not doing so, are not just personal preferences or personality styles (although our choices probably reflect those). The consequences of indirect forms of communication have a real-life negative impact on our relationships with others, and the effectiveness of the organization's functioning.

Consider the following results of indirect communication:

- Trust is undermined between coworkers and departments.
- Miscommunication occurs more frequently.
- Conflict increases and resentment grows between team members.
- Determining the source of problems becomes "fogged," and trying to solve them becomes a quagmire.
- An overall confusion is created across the organization.
- People choose "sides," and any sense of team cohesiveness is destroyed.

Sadly, all of these results are unnecessary. Fortunately, however, they also can be prevented.

THE OBVIOUS REMEDY:
COMMUNICATE DIRECTLY

As licensed mental health professionals, we (Jennifer and Paul) frequently experience the tension between healthy life practices being fairly easy to understand conceptually while at the same time being difficult to implement successfully (and consistently) in our daily lives. The same seems to be true with direct communication.

With a few possible exceptions, most people intellectually agree to the benefits of communicating via the established pathways within an organization, and to deal directly with a person with whom you are experiencing some challenges. But many of us do not actually *behave* in this manner.

The best way to pursue communicating directly with others is to identify and apply guiding principles that can direct you as you encounter various situations (the number of specific situations is too voluminous to address each of them individually).

- Commit to communicate directly with the person you should, even when it may feel uncomfortable or may lead to a negative reaction from them.
- Go through the proper channels of authority for requests, even if others don't or it isn't the "norm" within the organization.
- Be upfront about the situation and accept whatever responsibility you may have.
- Do not talk "through" others, either by using them as a messenger or informally sharing information, hoping they will pass it on.
- Avoid accepting the messenger role for someone else. Let them know they need to talk directly with the recipient.

Using these five principles will significantly reduce the amount of indirect communication in which *you* are involved, and will be a great starting point for others to see, and hopefully emulate, themselves.

DIRECT (EVEN BLUNT) COMMUNICATION WORKS

Nan was an accomplished professional who had worked in a position of authority for a high-prestige institution. In her previous role, she had directed projects and provided oversight to junior staff members. Intellectually bright, she was also a driven individual.

She was, however, in the midst of a career transition. Having moved to a new city as a result of her husband taking a leadership role in a national retail chain, she was in the midst of supporting her two oldest children who were finishing high school and looking toward college. But she also had time, interest, and energy to do some part-time consulting.

She joined a professional service organization that needed her skill set. Their work was of interest to her, being aligned with her personal values. At first, her responsibilities were clearly defined and related to specific projects. But over time, as she became more familiar with the goals of the organization and the leadership more clearly saw the depth of her competence and her ability to learn new skills, she started to have a broader reach into a variety of tasks.

On the one hand, this development was clearly valuable to the organization. Nan was able to plug into an ongoing project and provide needed expertise to help create more value or move the project along more quickly. On the other hand, she was *so* bright, competent, and self-directed that she started to function beyond the boundaries of her role—exploring additional resources to add to the project or to complete some tasks that were actually another team member's responsibility. Also, she tended to do this without communicating with Mike, the CEO to whom she reported, or anyone else on the team, until she announced what she had already done. Besides the boundary violations, this also incurred additional costs to the company for her services, which were billed hourly—potentially for tasks not needed or desired by the leadership team.

One day, in the midst of a project-based committee meeting, Mike, out of frustration with Nan doing tasks not asked of her, mentioned that, while her contributions to the project were helpful, he would like her to talk to him first before pursuing an idea she thought would be useful.

Shortly after the conclusion of the meeting, Nan briskly walked into Mike's office, stood over him and announced: "I have never been treated so rudely and disrespectfully in my career! I have overseen projects with a budget in the hundreds of thousands and had numerous team members report directly to me. I believe you owe me an apology for how you related to me in front of the team."

Mike, a bit taken aback by her reaction, first affirmed that he was sorry that his comment offended her, and that was not the intent of his comment. Seeking to more clearly understand what Nan was upset about, Mike asked her to clarify her perspective on what he had stated. When she had done so (and calmed down some in the process), he thanked her for talking directly to him and communicating her frustration. He then affirmed her value as a contributing team member and that he wanted to make things right with her; he asked for some time to think on the issue (his comment, her response, and the bigger picture) and committed to getting back to her within two days to talk further. She was fine with this process, and they had a follow-up discussion as promised.

Regardless of what you think about Nan's reaction (and how Mike handled the situation), the main point here is that her *talking to Mike directly*, even bluntly, provided the opportunity for the two of them to dialogue about the issue and, potentially, work out the situation.

On the other hand, Nan could have gone to one or more of the other committee members (or anyone else, for that matter) and complained: "Can you believe how Mike spoke to me in the meeting? What a jerk. Doesn't he know I've managed projects far bigger than this? I'm not far from marching in there, quitting, and leaving him high and dry." The problem is, that direction does not lead toward resolving the conflict.

Unfortunately, many people (for a variety of reasons) default to the indirect route. Complaining to another person may *feel* good for the moment (providing a sense of release from the venting), but doesn't provide an avenue for the resolution. What is Nan's colleague supposed to do? Agree with her? Try to correct her perception? Neither will lead to healing in the relationship.

For Group Discussion

1. *Which types of indirect communication do you observe in your workplace?*

2. *Which type is most disturbing to you?*

3. *Which of the various ways to communicate indirectly do you see yourself using at least occasionally?*

4. *What would be one action step you could take to move toward directly communicating with others?*

SECTION III

CHARACTER
AND CONFLICT

CHAPTER 6

TRUTH AND DECEPTION

YOU OPEN YOUR WORK EMAIL. Uh-oh. One from the boss. You take a deep breath and click on it. "Just following up on that report. How's it going? Anything else you need?"

You immediately respond. "Great! Everything's on track. Thanks!"

But it isn't quite on track. In fact, you're behind. But you're not going to tell the senior director that. Is that a "white lie" . . . or something darker?

"I remember getting pretty angry with our daughter when she was about five," said a mom we know. "She ate some candy—and lied about it. It wasn't the candy that bothered me. It was her not telling the truth. And I explained that to her." Most of us from the time we're small learn that lying is really bad. At the same time, we see it everywhere in our society and in the news. But how do questions of truth and deception play out in a work setting?

"Deception" is a word we try to avoid. Many react to its use in certain situations, saying, "I wasn't really *deceiving* them—that sounds almost evil. I just didn't tell them everything."

Our goal in addressing this issue is not to become anyone's conscience or the "moral police" on what is right or wrong. Neither is it our intent to try to resolve the millennia-long ethical dilemma whether there is ever an appropriate time and situation to not be totally truthful. We are well aware that our readers will have a wide range of positions on the issue—and to come to agreement on the answer to that question is not necessary to make our point.

Our position is this: at a minimum, telling the truth is preferable and leads to healthier interactions and relationships than not telling the truth. That is, from a practical point of view, when people within a workplace hold to the norm of speaking the truth to one another (as well as their customers and suppliers), a healthier workplace culture emerges. Conversely, if withholding the truth, giving partial information, or outright lying are acceptable ways of communicating, the organization and those who work in it will suffer.

Why? Because workplace transactions and relationships in general are built on trust. Without trust, organizations and people within organizations *cannot* successfully complete business transactions. Follow this example: You tell me of a need you have. I tell you that I can and will provide a service or make a product to meet your needs. In return, you will pay me (in a reasonable timeframe) for the goods and services I provide. This process requires trust by both parties.

The undermining of trust (by not fulfilling your part of the agreement) ultimately leads to the dissolution of the business relationship. If you don't build what I want, according to the specifications we agreed upon, or I don't pay you for your work, we cease to do business together. While deceptive practices in business can lead to short-term gains, they will not grow into a long-term mutually beneficial business relationship.

This goes back to the sayings of prior generations: "A man is as good as his word." Or, "We shook hands on the deal—that's good enough for me." (As opposed to the need to sign a detailed, legally binding contract.)

WAYS WE SHADE THE TRUTH

Part of the challenge of dealing with acts of deception in the workplace is that there are numerous forms. Some ways of deceiving others are more culturally accepted than others—for example, not speaking up when we are aware of another's false statements, in contrast to "bald-face lying" in response to a direct question. Also, certain types of deception are actually embedded in some cultures as virtuous (not telling the truth in a public situation to "save face" of a superior, or the value of being "shrewd" by not giving a purchaser the quality or amount of product they think they are buying.)

While we do not purport to have identified all types of deception that occur in workplace relationships, here are a number of the most commonly occurring ones:

- *Not following through on a commitment made.* "I'll have the draft of the presentation to you on Monday" (and then you don't).
- *Giving false information.* "Thanks for the order! We can get those to you by next Wednesday, no problem" (knowing that you can't, and it won't get there until later).
- *Withholding important information relevant to the situation.* "We have several Fortune 500 companies that have used our products" (but not telling them that: a) several were decades ago; and b) many were not pleased with the product and never reordered any).

- *Remaining silent when you know the other person is being deceived.* Listening to a more senior salesperson "over-sell" what your training program will cover and accomplish, and not giving the correct information to the potential client.

- *Making damaging (and untrue) implications to sway another.* "I tried to tell Phil that the programs wouldn't interface that way, but he insisted that it would and built the presentation assuming the components would work together fine" (when you were actually the one who came up with the idea initially).

- *Presenting inferior materials, products, or processes as being the same as ones previously agreed to.* "We can use a lower-grade material for the filling—they'll never know the difference."

Again, we acknowledge that there may be circumstances where one must struggle with an ethical dilemma of telling the truth or not, but we believe these situations to be extremely rare. The fact is that our desire to "bend" the truth occurs primarily to avoid negative consequences—to protect ourselves. For example, not admitting to a customer (and your supervisor) that they haven't received their order yet because you made a mistake in how you entered the order into the system.

Most daily workplace decisions are straightforward, and we hold to the position that communicating honestly is the best principle to live by. Others will learn to trust you, will grow in their respect for you, and your workplace communication will circumvent many challenging situations experienced by those who are less forthcoming in consistently telling the truth.

DEALING WITH DECEPTION IN THE SYSTEM

It's one thing to be personally honest. Unfortunately, however, there are instances when the team or organization we are a part of is intentionally engaging in deceptive practices. This leads to significant and serious ethical challenges in what is the appropriate action to take. This depends on a number of factors: your role in the organization, who has the authority within the organization to address the issue, and (potentially) the type of harm that may result.

Given the complexity and variety of situations, our best advice is:

- When at all possible, make sure your personal communication and actions with others are honest and trustworthy.
- Strive to influence those you work with toward honest communication, and advocate to the best of your ability to correct any wrongs resulting from prior deceptive practices.
- In situations where the issues are complex and your influence is partial or indirect, seek out wise counsel to think through the various options you have.

As you pursue these courses of action, you will become known as an individual committed to honest dealings, and those with differing values will be less likely to want to work collaboratively with you—making your choices and actions less difficult in the future. If you are in the unfortunate circumstance of working within an organization where their values differ greatly from yours, you may want to read our book *Rising Above a Toxic Workplace.*

For Group Discussion

1. *Are there any work situations where you think a partial truth might be preferable to total honesty?*

2. *What would you do if you found your organization was engaging in a pattern of deception?*

CHAPTER 7

SEEING THROUGH OTHERS' EYES

THOSE OF US OF A CERTAIN age remember the workforce of a long-ago era. "When I was little we would go pick up my dad at the commuter train from downtown," a friend recalled. "This was the '50s, and we'd watch for him amidst the sea of men in hats and suits and sometimes raincoats. They all looked exactly the same and then finally we'd be like, 'I see Daddy!'"

The world has changed drastically from those days, and today's organizations are diverse in every possible way. But even beyond surface differences, consider other reasons people you work with might view the world differently than you do:

- Growing up in a different era, culture, or subculture.
- Being raised in a family with different values, religious beliefs, and/or social, economic, or educational levels.
- Being shaped by personal experiences—moving, living in a different region of the US, family background, traveling to other cultures, even traumatic events.

While few people argue the point that each of us views the world from our unique perspective, often we don't stop to consider *how* different we are—partly because we don't know much about our coworkers' lives, current or past. As a result, we tend to assume that we all pretty much view the situation similarly, which is simply not true.

THE POWER OF PERSPECTIVE

Our perspective is like a lens through which we view and interpret what we are experiencing. Our viewpoint influences what we focus on in the experience—how we understand, synthesize, and respond to what we are "seeing." While we tend to believe that our perceptions are an accurate account of what is occurring, they actually *aren't* purely objective. How we experience a situation is influenced by our past experiences, prior knowledge, our beliefs about the world, and self-interest. That is why people tend to describe an event they experienced with others in sometimes vastly different ways—almost to the point that you wonder if they are describing the same event.

Understanding another's perspective is not just a cognitive process but also includes the ability to "read" another person's emotional state via their facial expressions, posture, gestures, tone of voice, and eyes. Research has demonstrated that we receive and decode these nonverbal messages more quickly than processing what a person says with their words, which means we tend to react to others' nonverbal cues first. The problem is we often misperceive and misinterpret these nonverbal cues, especially when our background and view of the world varies from our colleagues'.

WHEN NOT UNDERSTANDING ANOTHER PERSON'S VIEWPOINT CREATES PROBLEMS

We may not be aware of how important this skill is and the unnecessary problems that occur when we struggle in understanding others' view of situations. Here are some scenarios that are probably familiar to you:

A colleague reacts to the wording in a marketing piece, feeling like the words and images used are inappropriate and condescending. You are confused—not really understanding her concerns.

During a discussion among team members, a coworker expresses opposition to plans for a holiday celebration. His points seem off-target and tangential, and you really can't see what his objections are.

A supervisor who normally is even-tempered and inclusive in decision-making becomes uncharacteristically intense and dogmatic on his position during a team meeting. He says he is unwilling to consider other options. It seems that something "tripped his switch," but you are not sure what it was.

You and some of your coworkers are having an informal lunch together and start telling humorous stories about past events. Everyone seems to be enjoying the time, laughing together, when suddenly, in response to one story, one of the group appears disturbed, gets quiet, and then quickly gets up and leaves, saying, "You all are unfeeling and condescending toward anyone different from you. I can't take any more!"

When we are not able to see situations from another's point of view, bad things can happen. A short list of the consequences includes:

- Ineffective communication
- Consistently misinterpreting others' messages

- Difficulty in influencing others to see your point of view
- Leading others by "force" rather than influence
- Frustration that others don't understand or agree with you
- Frequent impasses in working with others rather than being able to "build bridges" and work collaboratively
- Unresolved conflicts
- Not understanding (or wanting to understand) those from a different background

If you (or others around you) often experience these outcomes, your ability to see or accept situations from others' perspective is almost certainly a challenge for you.

THE EMPATHY GAP

Children aren't innately empathetic. We try to teach them to share their toys, respond with concern when someone is hurt, offer someone else the last piece of cake, let another person decide what movie to watch. In the workplace it might mean understanding that some would rather not use their personal time for a holiday office gathering . . . or understanding that they do not celebrate that holiday.

Perspective-taking ability, as psychologists call it, is actually a skill that progresses over one's lifespan, moving from a viewpoint of "me" to "we" to "you" to "they." Unfortunately, a deficit in seeing another's perspective is a major problem within our culture. Within our society over the past several decades, the emphasis of parenting and education has been "me-centered." We teach children (who eventually become adults) to focus on themselves by asking: "What would *you* like to do?" and "Where do *you* want to go to eat?" There is nothing wrong with these questions by themselves. But when combined with the parenting approach of giving in to a child's desires when they say, "I don't want to!" and throw a major tantrum to get their way, we essentially teach them that the primary driving force for any decision is what *they* want to do—regardless of its impact on others.

This approach is in contrast to other cultures (for example, many Asian societies) in which one of the first questions considered is: *How will this impact my family and those close to me?* Additionally, the "me-centered" viewpoint leaves out the simple thought: *Maybe I should consider what others might want.*

REALITY 101

The ability and willingness to consider other people's point of view is based upon some foundational realities in life. Unfortunately, many employees (and leaders!) are still learning these reality-based facts:

1. You are not the only person in the world.
2. You and your preferences aren't the sole factor in making decisions.
3. Other people are different from you, they view life differently than you do, and these differences need to be considered in interactions and decisions.
4. To get along with other people collaboratively, you need to understand them (and they need to understand you).
5. Communication works best when you communicate in the ways other people think and communicate (rather than what makes sense to you).

The good news is, we can learn the skill of perspective taking.

HOW TO INCREASE YOUR
PERSPECTIVE-TAKING ABILITY

Developing the skill of seeing from another's perspective falls into the area of *emotional intelligence*. There are numerous helpful books and resources available to help us develop greater social and emotional understanding. Here are a few starting points to focus upon which can assist you in growing your ability to more accurately understand others and how they view life:

- Listen to others. Use active listening to check for accurate understanding of what they are sharing.
- Observe when people get upset or frustrated; seek to understand what is disturbing to them and how they are viewing the situation.
- Spend time with colleagues away from work; go to a recreational event of their choice (sporting event, concert, community event); meet their family and friends.
- Get to know more about your coworkers—where they grew up, important events in their lives, what they describe as important to them.

We are confident you will find that, when you take the time and energy to learn more about those with whom you work, you will understand them better—how they think, why they react to situations the way they do, and even why they choose the words and phrases they do in their communication. And when you understand them more fully, the miscommunication and misunderstandings between you will diminish significantly.

For Group Discussion

1. *In your experience, what causes the most misunderstandings among colleagues? Is it generational
   differences, cultural or political beliefs, or just the
   fact that each of us has our own perspective on
   things?*

2. *Have you noticed a trend toward people lacking
   empathy in your own workplace?*

SECTION IV

MAKING THINGS RIGHT WHEN YOU'VE MESSED UP

CHAPTER 8

APOLOGIZING IN THE WORKPLACE? REALLY?

WHEN WE TALK TO CLIENTS and friends in the business world about the idea of apologizing in the workplace, we get mixed reactions. Some are interested and supportive: "Really? That is *so* needed." Others aren't sure what to think: "Wow. I would have never thought of trying to 'go there' at work." And the final group thinks we're crazy: "Are you kidding? That's not even a consideration in the places where I've worked."

We understand. Apologizing and workplace relationships don't go together for a lot of people, but for others they are a natural combination. Why do we receive such mixed reactions? Let's start with those who just don't, or won't, apologize in a work setting.

WHY PEOPLE DON'T APOLOGIZE

What are the barriers to apologizing at work? First, *the process of apologizing is based on the belief that you may have done something wrong or inappropriate.* For some people, this doesn't fit with their worldview or possibly their view of themselves. Some people have a relativistic approach to behavior: what is "right" (or wrong) for you may not apply to me. We are different people, from different backgrounds, with different personality styles and values. So what is right or appropriate varies from person to person.

Others hold a similar but slightly distinct point of view—that behavior is really situation-specific. So whether an action is right or wrong largely depends on the circumstances surrounding the situation (thus, the name that is given to this viewpoint is "situational ethics").

Unfortunately, sometimes people are motivated to apologize out of external pressure from others. *They* don't necessarily believe they've done something wrong but they have been shamed by others. "I can't believe you did that! You need to go apologize to them *right now*!" Obviously, this impetus for apologizing often does not lead to the best results, since the action can be viewed as insincere, prompted only by guilt or embarrassment.

A different, but related, reason why some people don't see the need to apologize in work settings is because they believe they have never done anything wrong. That is, their reluctance is related to their view of themselves—that they are the brightest, most knowledgeable person on the team and their opinion (or way of doing things) is always right. (And if it isn't, it is either because you misunderstood them or someone erred by not providing them with all of the information to make an accurate judgment!) Anything that goes wrong cannot be their fault (by definition).

ADMITTING YOU'RE WRONG

A second barrier for some is the concern about *admitting* that they have done something wrong. This can come from a desire not to lose face in front of others (hurting their reputation) or feeling that owning up to a mistake will undermine their influence (or possibly their authority if they are in a position of leadership).

Such people may agree that what they did "wasn't the best" or that they should have acted differently. But acknowledging this fact to others (and worse, in public) is not an option for them. They typically see little benefit of doing so, and a lot of potential downside to admitting mistakes.

DISPLAYING WEAKNESS

Apologizing, for some, is an indication of weakness. In their view, to admit that they acted inappropriately and are seeking to rectify the situation with a colleague is taking a position that opens them up to all kinds of negative fallout. For many in the corporate world, any sign of weakness displayed makes you vulnerable to being ignored, set aside, stepped on, passed over, open to ridicule, and mocked. Essentially, your pathway to career advancement has been derailed. As a result, they have no interest in pursuing resolution to a conflict by apologizing.

"YOU LIED TO ME!"

Michael, a business consultant, had a disturbing interaction with a coworker, and he wasn't sure how to handle the situation.

Michael works for a small financial services firm that provides additional "value added" services to their clients, including business planning and human resource support. He is viewed as an important part of the team, to help market and bring client leads to the business.

Michael had been helping with some strategic planning for a small-business owner for several months. As commonly occurs, the business owner "went dark" for a few months while he was focused on daily operations and sales, so Michael had not met with him for a while.

One of Michael's colleagues, Jason, provides investment advising and various types of insurance coverage to the firm's business clients. He and Michael had talked briefly about Michael's client, and Jason asked Michael to introduce him to the client the next time they met. Michael agreed to do so.

In September, after not talking for three or four months, Michael met with his client to restart their planning process. During the meeting, the business owner informed Michael that he had already moved ahead with some of the plans they had discussed—hiring a new COO, and getting the business' "financial house" more in order. Part of this process included purchasing some comprehensive liability insurance to protect the company from any random lawsuits or claims placed against the company. As a result, Michael decided it wasn't appropriate to introduce the client to Jason (the company's other insurance needs were already taken care of).

Later that afternoon, after Michael's meeting with the client had concluded, Jason happened to stop by Michael's office. When he learned that Michael had met with the client and that Michael did not take the initiative to introduce Jason to the client, Jason exploded. "What? I can't believe this! You said you would introduce us! You *know* I've been waiting for the opportunity to talk with him about the company's insurance needs. You lied to me!"

Note that Jason was expressing all this while standing in the hallway outside of Michael's office, yelling loudly enough that everyone in their offices could hear. Jason continued to rant for about ten minutes, seemingly unwilling to hear Michael's account of the situation. Jason then stomped off in anger.

Michael wasn't sure how to respond. First, he was embarrassed by the publicly viewed confrontation (as were his other coworkers). Secondly, he felt torn. On the one hand, he did make a commitment to Jason to introduce him to the client. But on the other hand, the client no longer had a need to meet Jason.

After letting things settle overnight, Michael met with his supervisor (who had already heard about the blowup from other team members) to share about the experience and to gain some advice on what to do.

If you were Michael's supervisor, what would you advise him to do?

WHAT MAKES APOLOGIES SO IMPORTANT?

Humans have an innate sense of right and wrong. Making things right after an offense involves two things. One is apologizing and the other is forgiving. Every time we get offended, it creates an emotional block between us and them and the next time it happens another block forms until we have a big wall. It's very hard to talk through a wall, or around a wall and it doesn't go away just with the passing of time.

However, many organizations simply don't deal with hurt feelings and offenses. "Forgiveness in organizations received initial attention, but many organizational cultures seek to resolve hurt feelings and offenses through either putting the feelings on a shelf and trying to ignore them or submerging them in light of pursuing

conflict resolution or management strategies or seeking to recon-
cile regardless of whether forgiveness has occurred."[1]

GUILT, SHAME, AND APOLOGIZING

Someone has said, "Apologies are the Brussels sprouts of relationships."[2] But why do we feel that way? Here's another observation:

Apologies bring us face-to-face with the fact that we may have
done something wrong, have something to apologize for, triggering a sense of guilt and its close partner, shame. While it's true that
after an apology we tend to feel better and have a stronger sense
of integrity, the prospect of apologizing undermines the sense that
the apologizer is a good person. Saying "sorry" puts one's shameful
behavior out there for all (or at least the victim) to see.[3]

Effective apologies require vulnerability and they feel too risky
to some people. Men, especially, may have been raised on the belief that apology equals weakness. But the opposite is true. Think
about someone you admire. Can you picture them giving a heartfelt apology? Probably so. Why? Because we actually admire people who are strong enough to show some vulnerability by owning
up to their mistakes. TED speaker and researcher Brené Brown has
this to say: "Vulnerability is not winning or losing; it's having the
courage to show up and be seen when we have no control over the
outcome. Vulnerability is not weakness; it's our greatest measure
of courage."[4]

If I (Jennifer) could talk to that person in your office who
hasn't given a decent apology in the past decade, here's what I
would say: "You are crushing your credibility and trashing your
trust. This is stunting your career growth and causing untold
frustration for your work team." Our wish is to help people know
what to say whenever "sorry" isn't enough.

WHEN TO APOLOGIZE, WHEN NOT TO

Not every sticky situation calls for an apology. For example, an employee's feelings might be hurt by a bad work review. Is an apology needed? No. The truth is that some news is hard to share. Don't over-apologize in awkward situations in an attempt to make others feel better. Save your apologies for when you truly feel that you would have done something differently if you could have a do-over.

But when is an apology actually needed? The first step is to recognize that someone is offended. This leads to an often-difficult situation:

- What should I do when someone wants an apology but I don't think I did anything wrong?
- What if I was giving honest feedback and the other person became upset—do I owe them an apology?
- Does it matter whether every bit of what I said is true?
- What if they've had it coming for a long time?
- What if I'm an over-apologizer—how can I stop apologizing for every single thing that goes wrong at work?

And the most important question for an organization: How important is the relationship to us?

WHAT IF YOU AREN'T SATISFIED
WITH SOMEONE'S APOLOGY?

A number of years ago, my husband and I had an argument. The argument is only memorable because of what grew out of it. Being at fault that day, I shrugged and said, "Sorry" to J. T. while I was working in our kitchen. Next, I noticed that J. T. seemed unusually quiet during dinner. There was tension in the air, and a knot formed in my stomach. What my apology had lacked in elegance, I thought it made up in simplicity. Apparently not. So I asked him, "What's the matter?"

He said, "Well, I just wish you'd apologize."

I wanted to ask sarcastically, "What choo talkin' about, Willis? I said I was sorry!" But instead I quietly replied: "I *said* I was *sorry.*"

And then I got curious. I asked J. T., "What was I supposed to say?"

That's when I heard it. "Honestly, Jen, I wanted you to say you were wrong."

Wow. Looking back I realized that instead of making me guess what he needed to hear, J. T. had given me a gift in his answer.

What happened next? I said, "That's what I meant when I said, 'I'm sorry.' That is, I made a mistake and I was wrong." With that, the tension between us lifted like a fog rolling out to sea. We went on to have a happy evening, and I had my usually easygoing husband back.

This experience between us was directly related to my work as a clinical psychologist, and it sparked my research on apologies and forgiveness. I realized that J. T. is not alone. We all have scripts that come from our childhoods for apologies. But the trouble is, we have a glaring lack of awareness about *effective* apologies. I realized that J. T. and I were speaking different languages. And I thought there might be a lot of people in the same boat. So I reached out to Gary, an acquaintance at the time.

Gary and I began our meeting by reviewing his five love languages. They are: words of affirmation, quality time, tangible gifts, acts of service, and physical touch. What he says is that if you really want someone to feel loved or appreciated, you should not speak your own language, but you should speak theirs. Otherwise you're going to be wasting your effort.

Next, I told him about my apology breakthrough with my husband. I added that when it comes to apologies, the key word is *sincerity*. We want to know, "Do they really mean this or are they just trying to get this behind us?" I told him that I was struck by the similarity between the need to match up our apologies with what they expect and the need to match up love languages with what they expect.

Gary said he really resonated with the idea. "Yes, for any relationship to last beyond the initial infatuation stage, people have to be able to apologize. You don't have to be perfect. But you do have to deal with your failures effectively. Otherwise, you won't have good relationships."

That, we might add, is true in the workplace as well as in our personal relationships.

"MISSING IT"

Just like with expressing appreciation to a coworker, we agree that what one person considers to be an apology is not what another person considers to be an apology. People, even when they apologize, too often are "missing it" with each other because they have different ideas of what it means to apologize. If someone has hurt us and they're apologizing, in the back of our mind what we're asking is, "Are they sincere?" Because if we judge them to be sincere, we can forgive them. But if we think they're just trying to whitewash it, it's hard to forgive.

Wanting to obtain some real-world data, Gary and I sent out a survey on apologizing before we began working on the book. We noticed that the answers to our survey questions fell into five categories. We coined the term "apology languages" for these five different ways of saying, "My bad." You can think of these as separate languages or as steps that work together to build a great apology. In our experience, most people are satisfied with just one or two of these phrases for a simple mistake. But if the offense is either serious or repeated, they're really going to want to hear something more— preferably in their primary apology language. We've found that for most people, there is an apology language that's most meaningful to them across situations. Each apology language is a separate key. Taken together, they can unlock the door to the doghouse in which you may find yourself if you fail to help a coworker, insult a team member, fall short of expectations, or make other missteps.

THE LANGUAGES

Our first apology language is *expressing regret*. Some people most want you to say, "I'm sorry." But that is not a complete sentence. It's important that we give details to convey we understand their feelings, how we've made them feel—sad, angry, frustrated, worried. They need to know that we understand their pain. Regret focuses on what you did or failed to do, and how it affected the other person. They want some evidence that you realize how deeply you have upset them. For some people, this is the one thing they will be listening for—they need to hear you express regret. Otherwise, they won't feel that your apology is sincere.

Our second language is *accepting responsibility*. Some people most deeply want to hear the words, "I was wrong." Now, this is really hard for some people to say. Often our reluctance to admit wrongdoing is tied to our sense of self-worth. To admit that we are wrong is perceived as weakness. We may reason that only losers confess their mistakes; intelligent people try to show that their actions were justified. We may admit that what we did or said was not the best, but for many customers, the most important part of an apology is hearing that they have been wronged. It's what convinces them that your apology is sincere. As one man said, "'I'm sorry' is not enough. I want to know that they understand that what they did was wrong."

Our third language of apology is *making restitution* (or "making amends"). Some people really want us to ask them, "What can I do to make this right?" For them, talk is cheap. They want to see action that backs up your words.

The CEO of a digital marketing organization said this: "I've found the most important apology language to use in the workplace is making restitution. No matter what the error is, you have to work past mistakes when you're cooperating. In a workplace, that's inevitable. This means that you should try to include action steps with every apology. That's what people are listening for. When you follow up an 'I'm sorry' with 'and here's how I'm going to make it right,' they'll be far more willing to accept your apology and you'll be a stronger team down the line because of your actions."[5]

Our fourth apology language is *planned change*, saying, "I'll take specific steps (name them) to prevent a recurrence." Some people most want to hear us say what's going to be different going forward. They want to know that we've put some time and effort into making a better plan. When something didn't work, we should tell them, "Here's a new insight I have about where we went off-track. I can't promise I won't make another mistake, but here is my best plan for preventing us from ending up in this bad spot again."

Our fifth and final language of apology is *requesting forgiveness*. Some people most want to be asked this question: "Will you please forgive me?" Now, you may be thinking, "I've never asked that question! That would never even pop into my head!" But some people, through past experience or out of a certain moral sense or whatever the reason may be, may feel like we're stopping short of a true apology if we leave out that question. When we end our apology without asking for their forgiveness, they are left wondering, "Why did you stop?"

I (Gary) have to be honest with you. This one was not on my radar. I mean, I thought an apology was something you said; not something you asked. And anyway, wouldn't you automatically *know* that I want to be forgiven? Why would I be apologizing if I didn't *want* to be forgiven? But for some people, they're waiting for you to ask for their forgiveness. And in their mind, if you don't request forgiveness, you're not sincere.

THE APOLOGY LANGUAGES

1. EXPRESSING REGRET "I am sorry."

2. ACCEPTING RESPONSIBILITY "I was wrong."

3. MAKING RESTITUTION "What can I do to make it right?"

4. PLANNED CHANGE "I'll take specific steps to prevent a recurrence."

5. REQUESTING FORGIVENESS "Will you please forgive me?"

As we've all seen in recent years, there are sincere apologies and there are insincere ones—usually from some company that messed up and hires an outside PR firm to get out in front of the potential damage. Don't be that company. Each of these languages has its place in an organization—internally and externally—for employees, for boards, for suppliers, for customers and stakeholders, and even for the larger community.

For Group Discussion

1. What is the best thing people say or do when offering apologies?

2. What is the worst thing people say or do when offering apologies?

3. Does your workplace offer training on how to apologize in person, over the phone, or by video? Via email or text? Other?

4. Action step: Is there a coworker who might want to hear an apology from you?

CHAPTER 9

BEST PRACTICES (AND NOT-SO-GOOD ONES)

THE SCENE:

Dan is the COO of a small company in the western United States. He manages a staff of twenty with efficiency and care. He became frustrated over time with upper-level managers who brought requests to his administrative staff that were putting an undue burden on the team. A couple of these managers had developed a reputation for being a day late and a dollar short on meeting deadlines. They have the power to ask the administrative staff to accommodate their delays and small failures, but Dan's team was grumbling about all the pressure they were under. As a result, Dan has fallen into the role of being a bodyguard for the support staff. He functions as a "bouncer," guarding the inboxes and office doorways of the most stressed support staff members.

He makes general requests for the rest of the team to be mindful of how busy the support staff is and to not give them extra, unnecessary requests. These nonspecific requests don't seem to be doing the job, and the pressure has continued to mount on his associates.

THE INCIDENT

Dan sent out a routine poll to the whole staff asking for feedback within two days on a new program that they were all using. The timeline was short, but he felt it was reasonable. Most of the staff completed the quick poll and returned it to him. But one manager, whom we will call Monica, predictably didn't quite meet the deadline. By the time she sent in her survey, the staff had already tabulated the firm's results. Monica politely asked Dan whether the support staff could add her feedback into the group's results because she had strong feelings about the program. She apologized for having been late with her responses and tried to explain that she had been busy with clients over the intervening days.

Dan had a dilemma. Should he accept her tardy results and ask his support staff to integrate them? Or should he let Monica know that this was a classic example of a bad habit that he wanted her to break? If he did the former, Monica wouldn't be mad at him. But he would be extra-frustrated with her, and his administrative staff would continue to feel overextended. If the latter, Monica might feel hurt, and she might get mad at Dan. But things might improve going forward.

THE RESOLUTION

Dan took a deep breath and dove into some uncomfortable but necessary conflict. He called Monica on the phone (both of them were working remotely). This is what Dan said to her: "I don't like conflict. And it would be easier for me to let this slip by than to stop it. But I'm going to highlight this as an example of what I've been asking for. I want managers like you to be more careful about meeting deadlines and not asking the support staff to do extra work. Yes, your request would only take the support staff ten or fifteen minutes to complete . . . but they get multiple requests like this, and they have grown understandably frustrated over time. I'm usually accommodating, but this time I'm going to say no."

How did Monica respond? Dan was fortunate that Monica quickly understood his point. She has a high emotional IQ. She listened carefully, restated what she heard, and actually thanked Dan for his direct feedback. Although the conflict was uncomfortable for both of them, they are paving the way for continued openness and respect within their firm.

A final point: Dan could have told Monica no via chat or email. But his instincts told him that he should have the conversation in a way that would convey his tone of voice to her (and hers to him). What were his options? An in-person conversation, video call, or a telephone call. His choice allowed Dan to control the way in which Monica interpreted his message. His no might have been hard for Monica to hear, but it was a softer no because Dan showed caring and respect with his voice.

TALK IN PERSON

Do you have a hard topic to talk over with someone? Perhaps you need to circle back to a bad situation and offer an apology. Maybe you need to ask someone to act better next time. Whatever your challenging topic is, emails, texts, tweets, and messages via social media are likely to fail you. I (Jennifer) have seen the pitfalls of arguments via text or email so many times that I've created this rule for myself: Don't take the bait when a text or email thread turns negative. Keep electronic communication going as long as the topic is neutral or positive. But if the topic gets heated, reply only *one* more time. In that reply, say this: "I'd like to table this topic until it's possible for us to talk it over."

Why not make my very reasonable counter-argument on the spot? Here are my four reasons:

- Typed words on a tense topic invariably sound harsh. Even if you chose your words very carefully, they lack a gentle tone of voice to soften your message.
- They can't read your body language and see your caring expression.
- It's difficult, maybe even impossible, to gauge, while writing emails or texts, when to STOP. If your message is upsetting, you won't hear the protests from the other side, and you won't be able to adjust your words to fit their reaction.
- Texts and emails are too easy. Taking the time to talk to others will underscore your deep sincerity.

For dealing with awkward situations or when offering an apology, it's best to arrange to talk in person. If that isn't possible, pick up the telephone or hop on a video call with the other person.

What should you do if the shoe is on the other foot and you receive an email "bomb"? How can you begin to work things out? First, step away from the computer. Calm down, get into a peace-making frame of mind, then do what they should have done: reach out in person. Try saying this, "I appreciate where you're coming from, but I have a policy of not hashing out thorny issues via text or email. I value you, and I'd like to talk things over with you. What would be a good time for us to connect via phone, video, or in person?"

Have you heard about the epidemic of dating breakups occurring via text? This point might seem obvious, but here is an actual break-up text a young person showed to me (Jennifer). It said, "I just don't think this relationship thing is going to work." I was speechless. How does this problem translate to the workplace? Don't quit or fire someone via text. I understand that email is sometimes used in this capacity for ease of convenience or in order to have a record of your conversation. But it's best to handle the conversation one-on-one and to follow up with an email to cover your major points. In summary, don't hide behind digital media. It's both kind and respectful to reach out to others in person. When in doubt, use the Golden Rule: Do unto others as you would have them do unto you. Deal with problems directly, give people the benefit of the doubt whenever possible, and don't be harsh. Your colleagues will appreciate your efforts.

WRITE IT OUT

If you are going to offer an apology for a very serious offense, here is a suggestion: write out your apology. Then take it with you and share it with the offended party or parties. The time you took to write it will underscore your sincerity. Bonus: you won't forget anything that you wanted to be sure to include. Also, don't let yourself get distracted. So leave your cellphone behind when you head out to have a heart-to-heart conversation. If someone comes to your office to talk with you, turn off your computer monitor to signal that they have your undivided attention. And if you're talking things over via videoconference, don't try to multitask. People can tell when you're checking emails on the side. Instead, focus on your team without any distractions. This will pay dividends in terms of the team's trust, loyalty, and output.

THE BLAME GAME AND OTHER MISTAKES

Here are three defensive apology mistakes that people often make: Blaming others, excusing yourself, and denying the seriousness of your actions. Have you noticed that when something goes awry, the first thing many of us do is to try to subtly blame it on someone else? What makes blame so uncomfortable? Many people act as if getting blamed for something is the worst thing that could happen to them. In reality, it's far worse to become known as someone who tries to pass the blame to others—to throw coworkers under the bus. One of the most admirable things we can do is to hold up our mistakes and accept responsibility for them. When we do this, we build trust with others.

We also need to be careful not to make excuses for our actions. Benjamin Franklin said this: *"Never ruin an apology with an excuse."*

The word BUT is a red flag, warning that an excuse is on the horizon. "I'm sorry. But at the same time . . . " Or: "I'm sorry. If you . . ." (would only listen, would take responsibility, etc.). And don't say, "I'm sorry you feel that way." Both phrases are invalidating and they turn your apology, into a non-apology.[1]

An airline in America offered these words in their May 2018 apology for having questioned a Caucasian passenger about whether her biracial son was hers: "We apologize if our interaction made this family uncomfortable—that is never our intention."[2] Where did the company make a mistake? Raising the question "if" someone felt uncomfortable fails to acknowledge the pain that the person experienced. An apology cannot adequately serve dual purposes: it cannot simultaneously express regret for the pain caused and justify innocent intentions, as this apology attempts to do with the emphasis on "that is never our intention."

I (Jennifer) worked with a company that had an employee whom I'll call Sasha. She paid such close attention to every single detail that she was driving her work team crazy. One day, a coworker whom I'll call John blew up at her, which was not unusual for him. But then John came to Sasha the next day and started to give her a quasi-apology. He said something like, "Sasha, I shouldn't have said what I said to you—but you really should loosen up."

Sasha stood firm, reminding John of his past jabs. "Stop blaming *me* for *your* anger issues," she said.

Also, don't try to defend your good intentions, saying something like "I didn't mean to . . ." Instead, focus on the other person and how he or she was affected by your choices. It's so easy to rationalize, to deflect, to cover ourselves, to try to make ourselves look good at all times, whatever the cost.

But no one is relationally perfect. You will make mistakes. Don't expect your colleagues to just accept you as you are. Show that you are willing to make changes to do better the next time.

"I JUST WANT TO GET IT OVER WITH"

Many people are conflict-averse and want to get an issue settled quickly so that things can "get back to normal." They are willing to accept responsibility and apologize even if they do not sense that they are at fault, simply to get the issue settled. They don't like the emotional discomfort that comes from long, honest discussions about the issue. They would much rather apologize, accept the responsibility, and hope that they can move on.

Jonathan is thirty and really enjoys his job. "I don't always have to win, and I don't like confrontation. I will apologize even if it is not my fault, because I want to move on. I don't want to waste time arguing."

A "PEACE" THAT LEADS TO RESENTMENT

Many individuals desire peace at any price. They will take the blame, however undeserved, just to put an end to the conflict. Emotional calm is more important than being right. While this may appear to be an admirable trait, it often simmers as inner resentment.

Sam and Paula have been co-owners of a franchise for fifteen years. Sam said, "I'm the one who seems to apologize most in our partnership. Paula isn't good at verbalizing her feelings. And in order to get past whatever it is that went wrong and caused hard feelings, I usually end up apologizing just so we can get back on speaking terms again. I often end up internalizing hard feelings because I have to apologize, even when I'm not the one who caused the problem."

Such internalized resentment often creates emotional distance within teams. On the surface things seem to be relatively calm, but underneath an emotional explosion is in the making.

If a person senses such emotional resentment building, it is time to talk to a coach or a consultant. Failure to process resentment can lead to the destruction of both small teams and entire companies. Peace at any price is not the road to authentic relationships.

RELATIONSHIP REPAIR

Apology alone does not restore a relationship. There has to be a response to the apology. Sometimes, not always, the response is to forgive or just say, "No worries." But if someone has been really hurt by something that happened in their work setting—

anything from being passed over for an important committee to being dressed down in public—the relationship is going to need to be repaired. An apology won't go far enough.

If you're the one who's been offended and the other person is apologizing to you, but not in a way that really connects with you, you now understand that there are five different apology languages and you know what they are. It makes it easier for you to ask for the specific type of apology that you would like to hear. But if that feels too uncomfortable to you or if your request is unsuccessful, you have another option. You can attempt to forgive them even if they're not apologizing in your preferred way. You can say to yourself, "Okay, they're saying, 'I'm sorry.' That's not really what I want to hear. But I know that is one way to apologize." Keep your mind open and be ready to forgive the other person. And if no apology is forthcoming, let it go. (We will have more to say about that later.)

If you're the offender, you need to make things right—through apologizing but also through other actions designed to restore trust. If the two of you need to work together regularly, you will need to move through the conflict and hurt and find healthy ways to function as colleagues.

THE OFFENDED CUSTOMER

Offenses are inevitable. They happen. And when a customer is offended, consequences can be severe. Customer loyalty is eroded or even erased. An offended customer feels that a trust has been broken. Offending a customer creates a barrier, which will obstruct a shared future. A key step to restore trust and rebuild loyalty is an effective apology. I (Jennifer) have a friend who heard my book title and immediately said, "But I don't *want* to apologize." In reality, apologies are healthy. They are not symbols of weakness.

When we offer them, they come from a place of strength and confidence. With an apology to a customer, you recognize that they have a need for justice—and you have an opportunity to right a wrong.

Before you wrap up your customer service apology, try this. Say, "Here's what we can do for you. . . . How does that sound?" Then ask, "Is there anything else in your experience with us that didn't please you?"

Taking these steps can turn an unhappy customer into a loyal customer.

Next, work with your team to figure out what is causing problems and how they can be prevented in the future. In military parlance, the After Action Review (AAR) is one of the most effective tools to help improve literally all aspects of the organization. You want to work with your organization to stop problems from happening repeatedly. Just as saying how you will prevent a recurrence is a key step in apologizing, putting your heads together as a team will pay big dividends.

There is great value in extending apologies outside the company to customers and to the public. Some companies give mixed messages to their employees about owning up to mistakes, as they protectively deny or hide their mistakes. When they can't hide a mistake any longer, forced apologies lack sincerity. But when companies retain the trust of their customers, they have valuable brand ambassadors.

For Group Discussion

1. *How have you seen aversion to conflict play out in your organization?*

2. *Is it hard for you as an employee or manager to own up to mistakes? What are some examples you have seen of companies that had a hard time admitting fault?*

3. *What cultural differences have you seen in the ways apologies are given and received?*

CHAPTER 10

WHY APOLOGIZING DOESN'T RESOLVE EVERYTHING

WHEN WE HAVE HAD A CONFLICT or disagreement with someone at work, often a sense of tension lingers, clouding the relationship. The expression of this tension looks different depending on the circumstances, the type of relationship you have with them (close or casual), and the personality styles of each individual.

Sometimes the tension builds and can lead to an angry exchange. In others, a cool distancing develops—the two parties avoid one another, rarely communicate, and when they do, the interaction can be quite frosty. In both cases, the relationship has suffered.

Even when an apology has been offered and possibly accepted, additional steps may need to be taken in order to make things right between two people. That is, apologizing by itself does not necessarily resolve all of the issues created by the initial offense. This dynamic is especially true when one or both of the parties have been hurt and were deeply offended by the actions of their colleague, or the actions have been longstanding and repetitive.

Eric and James had worked together on the same IT team for several years, but had different roles and responsibilities. Given that they worked in a small department, they often would help one another on various daily tasks, covering for their colleague when one of them was swamped completing a large project or dealing with a high volume of internal requests for help. This arrangement generally worked well, but recently they had both felt stretched by the amount of work they had to do. When Eric asked James for his help finishing a report on cybersecurity that was due imminently, James said, "Sorry, man. I'm pretty busy this week. Ask Ravi."

While the message was accurate factually, James's response was very out of character for him. Eric said, "Yeah . . . okay," and went to find Ravi.

The next morning, James approached Eric and apologized. "Hey, Eric, I'm sorry I kind of blew you off yesterday. I'm trying to get this one thing done before vacation, and I've been pretty stressed out. Do you still need my help?"

Eric said, "No, I'm good, but thanks." Yet he was still a little confused by James's seeming brush-off. He and James had been friends for years—in fact, he had recommended James for the position. James had always had his back. Eric wasn't the type to stew over things, but something was off here.

For his part, James felt a little rebuffed. He had reached out to Eric, said he was sorry, but he knew his friend well enough to sense that things weren't quite right yet.

When there has been a conflict at work, one challenge in making things right is that resolving issues involves a multiple-step process. The second difficulty: often, we aren't in control of all of the pieces—the process involves others, and they may not be willing to immediately do what is needed on their end.

We can take responsibility for an error we made, ask forgiveness and offer to make restitution, but if the other (offended) party is not willing to accept our apology and move on, the process can become stuck and the relationship will still feel tense.

TOO BIG TO FAIL?

Most of the focus of this book has been on interpersonal situations between two people. But in the workplace there are some conflicts that involve a group of people versus one coworker. Consider the following example.

Carl was a minority owner in a small business that sold insurance. The company had fifteen employees. Carl produced about half of the revenue of the company and more than half of its internal turmoil. He was prone to fits of anger. He singled out employees and berated them. Carl was accusatory, intimidating, loud, shaming, and rude. Later, he would calm down and try to move on, but he never apologized. So everyone avoided working with Carl. He went through assistants at a rate of two or three per year. If he had been in a large company with a functioning human resources department, he surely would have been fired. Instead, the majority owner (Greg) offered Carl a deal: stay on as a consultant and be paid handsomely to grow your silo. Stay out of the firm's management. This arrangement worked for a couple of years. Carl's clients loved him. They thought he was a wonderful, nice man. His coworkers knew that Carl was a Jekyll-and-Hyde character.

The employees complained to Greg about Carl's ongoing mistreatment of them. They pushed Greg to fire Carl, but Greg refused to do so for financial reasons. From the perspective of their lucrative client relationships, Carl was "too big to fail." So Greg became the monkey in the middle: He *could* fire Carl, but he would not agree to do it. About once per year, Greg would confront Carl, telling him that he needed to stop having angry outbursts at work and stop running off his assistants.

Everything changed one day when Greg confronted him in the usual way. Carl responded impulsively by submitting his resignation in anger. Greg was nervous about clients leaving the firm, but Carl honored his noncompete agreement and most of his clients remained with the company. The employees held their breath, hoping and praying that Carl would not attempt to undo his resignation when he calmed down. To their delight, he actually departed. Within a year, the company had replaced the clients that left when Carl exited the agency. The company continues to grow and today is thriving. New employees came on board when the company expanded from two to three locations. To this day, the employees who worked with Carl shake their heads with dismay when his name comes up.

CHANGING THE LANGUAGE
AROUND FORGIVENESS

One "elephant in the room" that gets in the way of mending relationships is the fact that, for many people, forgiveness in the workplace is a foreign concept. They view forgiveness as primarily a religious or moral matter that really doesn't fit or apply to their life and relationships at work, or something better applied to personal situations, such as forgiving a spouse who wrongs you, or forgiving your parents for long-ago hurts.

As a result, we want to suggest an alternative term that, in the context of workplace relationships, can convey similar meaning. That term is *letting go*. As mental health professionals, we are well aware of the damage that occurs when we choose to hold onto resentment toward others. The resentment and bitterness keep us agitated internally and almost "eats us up" from the inside out— we lose sleep, our blood pressure rises, we have an upset stomach, or we experience headaches and back pain from the tension we are carrying. Learning to "let go" is a better pathway, so let's explore what it means to do so and also debunk common misconceptions about the meaning of "letting go."

For Group Discussion

1. *What is your gut reaction to the word* forgiveness?

2. *Have you ever had a toxic boss or one who was "too big to fail"? If so, how did you handle it?*

3. *With hindsight being 20/20, how do you wish you could have managed a difficult or toxic work situation in the past?*

LETTING GO OF PAST HURTS

CHAPTER 11

UNDERSTANDING "LETTING GO"

THROUGHOUT THIS BOOK WE'VE been looking at ways to "make things right" when conflict happens among work colleagues. Whatever the conflict is, whoever is involved, we cannot resolve it unless we are able to let go of hurt, anger, fear, bitterness, and the other emotions that get hold of us. The process of letting go—releasing the desire to gain retribution or revenge to someone who has offended you—is considered by most mental health professionals to be foundational in order to "move on" in one's life. The concept and process is complex and often misunderstood, so let's break it down in a series of components.

The need to let go occurs when we feel hurt, embarrassed, let down by another, offended, angry, and disappointed. These responses are the result when someone's actions (or lack of action) are in contrast to what we believe *should have* happened. That is, we have negative feeling responses when our expectations aren't met by another.

Sometimes we need to check our expectations: were they realistic? But, for this discussion, we will assume that the expectation was agreed upon by both people (such as a due date for a report) or is consistent with social norms (for example, not yelling and calling someone names in the midst of a group meeting).

WHAT HAPPENS WHEN WE DON'T LET THINGS GO?

The most obvious result of continuing to hold onto hurt and anger from the past is the ongoing tension in the relationship with your coworker. There continues to be a relational break that creates challenges in communicating, working together, and makes those around you feel uncomfortable.

Possibly the more important consequences are the costs to *us* internally. We ruminate about the offending event, which creates agitation, both emotionally and physically, within us. We hold conversations with others about that person. We avoid the other person. We become increasingly angry. We become obsessed about "getting even." All of our interactions with the individual are influenced by the hurtful event. The relationship is increasingly damaged. We create a negative, uncomfortable working environment. Ultimately, we become miserable.

WHAT LETTING GO IS NOT

Just as important as defining what the process of "letting go" looks like is to also describe what it isn't. First, *excusing the person's behavior* is not part of getting past the event(s). Saying, "That's okay;" "It's no big deal;" "Don't worry about it" are *not* part of the process. We are not absolving them of the responsibility for their actions. Often, what they did was clearly wrong, and we should not tacitly say the action was okay when it wasn't.

Secondly, "letting go" is not *forgetting what was done to you.* You might have heard people say, "If you haven't forgotten, you haven't forgiven." That's not true. Everything that you've ever done and everything that has ever been done to you is recorded in the human brain, although the memory is not always in the conscious brain. Sometimes it's in the subconscious. But sometimes what happened in the past will come back to your memory, even after they've apologized—*if* they apologized. Often, even after you have forgiven them, the memory of what they did will come back to you. And with the memory often comes emotions. So letting go does not destroy all the painful emotions. When you remember what they did, the painful emotions often come back. It may be anger, it may be hurt, and it may be disappointment—whatever words you give to it—but your emotional reactions return. If so, tell yourself, "Yes, I remember the offense. Yes, it hurts again, but I'm not going to let it control me."

Also, the process of letting go *does not remove all the consequences of poor choices.* When we internally let go of our resentment or anger, the practical consequences of what happened remain. A client said this to me (Gary) about a big problem: "Dr. Chapman, I've got to be honest, I have forgiven him. But to be very honest, I don't trust him." And I said, "Welcome to the human race. Forgiveness does not automatically rebuild trust. But forgiveness opens the door to the possibility that trust can be rebuilt."

Related to this, *total healing of the damaged relationship may or may not be a part of the process.* Even though complete restoration of the relationship would be a positive result, this often is not the case. Just like apologizing does not necessarily restore a damaged relationship to wholeness, neither does the healthy process of our letting go of our hurt feelings. This is an important point to emphasize because some people have unrealistic expectations, believing that "If I do A, B, and C, everything will be as good as new." Reconciliation between two people is clearly possible, but a full restoration of the relationship to its prior state of health may be difficult (depending on the level of offense that occurred).

WHAT LETTING GO INVOLVES

There are three components to the process of letting go—and we must remind ourselves that it is a *process*, not a "one and done" decision. Time is required to reflect, process what has happened, and to release our desires and feelings.

First, *we acknowledge that the other person is human*. We all are. That is, we all react in ways we shouldn't at times. Each of us makes mistakes and has errors in judgment. Everyone has some character trait (for example, impatience or impulsivity) that we need to work on. This includes the person who has offended you, and it is part of the nature of reality as we know it.

Next, and this seems to be a difficult step, is *surrendering your right to get even*. This can mean giving up your desire to see them hurt (emotionally or in their career) or a deep longing that bad things will happen to them. Wanting to get back at them and scheming about ways to do so is another variation. Again, it is important to remind ourselves that we are *not* saying what they did was okay, or that they should be rescued from any natural consequences that may occur from their actions. Rather, we are giving up *our* "right" to cause them pain in response to what they did.

The third step is to begin to *revise your feelings toward the person*. This takes time. You may react, saying to yourself, "I can't change my feelings! They are what they are." Addressing this issue fully is beyond the scope of this chapter, but excellent research demonstrates both that: a) we *are* in control of our feeling responses; and b) there are practical steps that can be taken to help in the process of changing how we feel about others or situations.[1] The key is to begin to change the statements you say to yourself about the person and/or situation. For example, "Yes, Jan said some hurtful things to me in front of others, but I want to move on and work to rebuild a positive relationship with her."

BASIC TRUTHS OF LETTING GO

As we work the process of getting past the difficult situations from the past, we need to remind ourselves of some foundational principles. In these circumstances, *we are dealing with persons for what they do, not who they are.* All of us at times make decisions and display behaviors that are inconsistent with "who we are" (or who we would like to become) and are discordant with the values we say we hold. Relating to one another with grace allows each of us the opportunity to change and grow.

Another foundational truth is that *we can let go even if people wound us.* If this weren't the case, no hope would exist for any of us to get past the difficulties of life in a healthy way. Life includes hurts, disappointments, and, unfortunately, wounds—physical, emotional, and relational. Thankfully, we can move beyond these hurtful experiences and continue on a positive pathway in life.

Lastly, we *can let go even when people have wronged us.* Some hurtful situations and actions are unintentional or a result of miscommunication and misunderstandings. Others are the direct result of malintent and the desire to hurt, damage, and even destroy others. Many times, working through the process of giving up the desire to see the perpetrator "get what they deserve" is challenging when it seems clear their actions were intentional. Fortunately, even in these difficult circumstances, their actions and desires don't have to control us in the future.

WHO IS LETTING GO REALLY FOR?

By now, the initial answer should be obvious: *for you.* When we choose to give up our desire to "get even," the benefits to us are significant. We sleep better, we hold less tension in our bodies, we experience less physical symptoms (headaches, upset stomach, muscle aches), and our outlook and demeanor toward daily life improve. We can now see (and experience) the good things around us in our daily lives. Each of us (the authors) desire these results in our lives . . . and in yours.

As they say on game shows and late-night commercials, "But wait! There's more!" In addition to the internal, personal benefits we experience, other positive results also follow. First, there is less tension in the workplace. You may or may not realize this, but when you and a colleague are at odds with one another, the tension radiates out and affects those around you as well—your colleagues, your administrative assistant, supervisor, and possibly your vendors and customers and other stakeholders. When you work on resolving your frustrations, those with whom you work benefit.

Finally, when you are able to move on from the relational trauma and difficulties, you'll begin to see that both you and your team become more productive. You (individually) will have more energy and will be able to focus on the task at hand, rather than have invasive thoughts and feelings distract you. And your team will not have to "walk on eggshells."

THE HARDEST SITUATIONS

Two particularly difficult situations need to be mentioned because they can become sticking points in the process of making things right at work.

"Letting go" when people do not say they are sorry or show re-morse. The hard truth is that many workplace cultures do not much value the "soft skills" of empathy, kindness, and under-standing, let alone admitting we have intentionally or unthink-ingly caused another person pain. Also, some people simply have low emotional intelligence. You may have a boss or coworker or supervisee who fits that profile.

Whatever the reason, the reality is that the offending person may never apologize. Or if they do, it might feel perfunctory rather than heartfelt. You have to work with this individual on a daily basis, so what do you do to let go of the resentment that still simmers? You may find you need to reach out for help—outside the organiza-tion. Seek out a trusted friend or a counselor—and move on from the hurt.

Learning to "let go" with ourselves. We *all* make mistakes. And when we say something we shouldn't have, react inappropriately, or make a "stupid" decision, sometimes the hardest person to for-give is oneself. But we deserve forgiveness as much as anyone, and we don't need to beat ourselves up. So don't forget to apply these principles to yourself as well.

THE ONLY WAY

"Letting go" is the only way to maintain our sanity and our emo-tional health when we have had hurtful interactions with others. And unfortunately, conflict, challenging events, and difficult peo-ple are part of the reality of work (and of life in general). While the process takes time, the results are clearly worth the effort—espe-cially when you consider the alternative. Few of us want to live our life with accumulating unresolved conflict and even trauma, and the physical and emotional toll they take on us. Living in freedom from past wounds is a tremendous gift.

For Group Discussion

1. *Is there a situation you've had a hard time letting go of? If so, what methods for letting go have you tried? Have any of these worked?*

2. *Sometimes we feel pushed by others to let go of a problem before we're ready to do so. Have you ever felt pushed in this way?*

3. *What helps you to let go and move on?*

BUILDING AND REBUILDING TRUST IN RELATIONSHIPS

CHAPTER 12

UNDERSTANDING THE NATURE OF TRUST

FOR LIFE TO WORK, WE HAVE TO TRUST. Trust is critical for any functional relationship—but we're not very good at building and maintaining trust over time.

One employment expert said, "For so many years, we've avoided critical topics in the workplace, and it inadvertently created cultures of silence and avoidance. But it's not something that people are inherently good at doing. Leaders need the skills to effectively facilitate these conversations and the competency to manage conflict in ways that build—not break—trust."[1]

The issue of trust—and mistrust—is powerfully relevant in our culture today. We hear comments about trust all over the news and frequently in personal conversations: "I trust that guy about as far as I can throw him." Or: "I would trust her with my life." Or: "You can't trust (the government, Big Tech, vaccines, media, etc.)." You can't trust that bad actors out in cyberspace won't steal your identity, so you dutifully go through two-factor authentication to get to your banking information. Relationships founder on the rocks of broken trust all the time. Whole societies can struggle when trust is lost.

Trust is essential to work-based relationships for many reasons, including effective teamwork, smooth functioning of the organization to produce goods and services, better customer relationships, and, ultimately, optimal financial outcomes. However, we also need to remember that trust is a two-way street. Obviously, we desire for our colleagues and clients to trust us, but we also need to trust them. If we don't, we are not likely to delegate any tasks to them, and we will feel a need to "check up" on them to make sure they are getting things done on time and at the quality level we expect. This process will wear us out, because essentially we are taking responsibility for their work as well as our own.

Ultimately, trust is foundational to business transactions. When we enter into discussions with potential customers or clients, we try to assure them that what we are saying is true—that our product does what we say it does, that we can and will deliver the services they desire, and that the products or supplies they are purchasing from us are the quality we have agreed to.

Conversely, when we provide supplies or enter into a contract for a range of services over time, we are trusting that they will pay us (and in a timely manner) for the goods and services agreed to. Historically, a lack of trust between business entities has been one of the sources of tension and conflict between countries and governments.

The reasons why there seems to be an epidemic of distrust are a complicated discussion in and of themselves. But let's first understand what "trust" really is, so we can think, talk, and respond accurately to relevant situations.

TRUST IS NOT EITHER/OR

The issue of trust is not as clear-cut as we think. Making an "all or nothing," either/or judgment about whether someone is either totally trustworthy or they cannot be trusted at all is rarely valid. In reality, almost everyone can be appropriately trusted to complete *some* tasks successfully. Unfortunately, we tend to communicate in blanket statements ("I don't know what it is, but I just don't trust her") that feed into this type of binary thinking.

The reality is: *trust exists on a continuum.* You may have worked with me for a few years and know I strive to be an honest and ethical person. So you feel comfortable trusting me to pick up some lunch for you, and bring you the change. But you don't know me well enough to sign over all responsibility for your personal finances to me. It isn't that you don't trust me; you just don't trust me *that* much (yet). This is reality-based—there are different levels and amounts of trust within our various relationships.

TRUST IS SITUATION-SPECIFIC

We trust someone to be able to do a specific task. For example, if you were to trust me to fix your car, your trust would be misplaced because I have virtually no mechanical abilities at all. However, if you believed that I could type your paper for you relatively quickly, assuming I had the time, that would be a good situation in which to trust me.

The reason that it is important to understand that trust is situation-specific is because we then have a pathway to take in order to build or rebuild low levels of trust. If we just say, "He isn't trustworthy," there is nothing the other person can do to remedy the situation. Your statement is based on a personal judgment you have made and, essentially, "the case is closed." The topic is not up for discussion or a vote. The primary problem is that this type of approach leaves no path for correcting the situation.

Also, a vague "I don't trust them" absolves the person making the statement of any personal responsibility. They have an opinion, and there is nothing required of the speaker. It is like saying, "He's a jerk." A judgment is made, and there is nothing I need to do. This typically isn't helpful in building relationships. When we believe the other person is the source of the problem and that the issue only will be resolved when they change, not much good can happen.

CREATING SITUATIONS OF TRUST

When we understand that trust is situation-specific, then a relationship can move beyond the "all or nothing" impasse (she's trustworthy/not trustworthy). I can now say, "I trust John to be able to drive me to the airport and get me there on time," even though I may not trust him to manage my personal finances. So when we are having difficulty in trusting someone for a certain task, it can be helpful to identify situations or tasks for which you *can* trust them and proceed in that area. This is especially relevant when dealing with new colleagues or those who are still learning their job—give them a task that you believe they can do.

THE THREE C'S OF TRUST

Trust has three foundational components: competence, consistency, and character.[2] They are like the legs on a three-legged stool; without all three being present, the chair falls over.

Competence—If a person or business doesn't have the ability to do the task you desire, it is foolish to trust them to do so. Having the knowledge, ability, resources, and capacity to complete a task is at the foundation of trust. This is why testimonials, references, or endorsements from prior customers are so important—they provide external evidence to the claims of the service provider or manufacturer.

Key Question: Do they have the skill, training, and ability to do the task?

Consistency—A person or an organization may have the competence to complete the task; they have the skills, talent, and expertise to do what is expected. But if their products are of inconsistent quality, if they cannot consistently get the product to you on time, or if they as a service provider don't show up, it doesn't do you much good. In many service sectors, there are plenty of competent technicians, but if you don't know if or when they will come to do the work, you are not able to depend on them.

Key Questions: Are they available? Do they show up? Do they complete the task?

Character—In this context, character primarily refers to honesty, integrity, and the belief that the other person is considering your needs as well as their own. Trust in business dealings (especially complex ones) often relies on the party's willingness to trust that the information being given is true, there is nothing important being hidden or left out, and that the other party is not just wanting to make a "fast buck," but that they actually will deliver the goods or services they are promising.

Generally speaking, it is acceptable for an individual or a company to look out for their own interests—after all, they have to make money to stay in business. However, you want to know they are not only looking out for themselves, but are considering your needs and desires as well.

One word of caution: if your lack of trust in the person comes from the area of character, and specifically in the areas of honesty, integrity, or their being concerned about what is best for you, then be careful. Go slowly in trusting them.

Key Questions: *Do they take your (or others') interests into consideration? Or do they seem to be primarily self-interested?*

WHERE MISTRUST COMES FROM

But why do we not trust someone—or they us? There are, as you might expect, many reasons. "Because they're a bad person" is usually not one of them., although that often is how we feel or what we communicate to others. The reasons we may be reluctant to trust another person can come from:

Lack of clear communication—A simple misunderstanding of what was said or meant leads one party to believe the other person is not telling the truth.

Mismatch of expectations—The customer expects "A" quality for the price paid, while in our mind they paid for "B" quality.

Competency has not been demonstrated—We aren't sure whether the other person can really deliver the service because we haven't seen them do it.

Inconsistent behavior/performance—A team member is competent and has good intentions, but for unknown reasons, they aren't able to consistently provide what is needed.

Issues caused by external factors—A few examples might be: disruption of the supply chain to provide the materials needed, personal illness, a death in the family, new rules and regulations.

Misunderstanding the other person's intent—Mistakenly attributing malicious intent or ulterior motives leads to distrust.

Guilt by association—You are a business associate of a person with whom they have had prior negative interactions.

Others we trust report a negative experience with the person—One of your good friends had an unpleasant business dealing with the supplier you are considering.

MISTRUST IN WORK RELATIONSHIPS

There are so many potential areas for struggling to trust others at work. But certain themes do recur across work settings. Commonly reported situations where one person doesn't trust another often include concerns about the other person:

- not telling the truth, or withholding information
- not accomplishing the task on time
- delivering unacceptable work
- not keeping information confidential
- showing up at meetings late and unprepared
- undercutting you, gossiping, or spreading rumors about you

Trust and Following Through on Commitments

In your relationships, do you sometimes feel like you are between a rock and a hard place? Do people hide their disapproval about a decision at first but then act angry later on? Do you wonder what people really mean when they tell you yes? If people assure you they'll take care of a project, can you really trust them to follow through? Are they going to blame you if things turn out badly? Do people act frustrated and leave you wondering, "What did they mean by that comment?"

All of these are issues related to trust. Can you trust what others say? Can they trust you to communicate what you really think? None of us are mind readers; we need to be able to rely on each other's words and trust each other's actions. One remedy is to strive, and encourage your team members, *to say what you mean, and mean what you* say (which sometimes includes not saying anything!).

When You Don't Follow Through . . .

Sara is a partner in a small business. She and her business partner, Jon, keep arguing about little things. As I listened to Sara describe their latest blow-up, I heard something all too familiar these days: Jon had said he would follow through on a task, but nothing had been done yet.

Sara's problem began several months ago when Gus, an important link in their supply chain, had asked Jon to call him that week. Jon agreed to make the call but two weeks passed and he had not done so. Sara was beyond frustrated. First, she wanted Jon to do what he had agreed to do. Second, this had happened before with Jon. Now he was letting her down again, and he didn't seem to care at all. Third, Sara felt that she could not make the call on Jon's behalf without stepping on his toes. Further, Sara was tired of picking up the slack when Jon procrastinated. Sara's mind ran through all the times he had agreed to do something but had never followed up. Here is the troubling path her thoughts followed:

> Was he saying yes just to appease her, while never intending to keep his word?
>
> If he didn't keep his word, could she trust him?
>
> If she couldn't trust him, was their working relationship over?

Meanwhile, if you were Jon, confronted by your angry boss, your mind might swim with questions like these:

What is she so upset about?

Why does she go from 0 to 100 on her anger scale?

Can't she understand how busy I am?

Doesn't she know that I was just about to do what she had asked me to do?

To Jon and the millions of others who are like him, we'd offer this simple advice: Let your yes mean yes. If you won't do something, don't say you will do it. Handling the reaction that might arise from saying no can be difficult, but it will not be as great as the damage that results from repeatedly letting others down and being viewed as untrustworthy.

Sometimes renegotiating the timeframe by when the task will be completed is necessary. External circumstances can occur which make getting the job done when promised (the printer breaks down). Or other higher priorities might have come to light (solving a problem for your top client). Getting back to your colleague and letting them know about the challenge that has occurred and working together to find an acceptable solution is better than not communicating anything or letting things slide.

What became of Sara and Jon? The last we heard they were still at an impasse. Jon had not called Gus, but he also did not tell Sara that he wouldn't complete the task. Sara no longer trusts Jon to do what he says he will do. They are drifting, frustrated, unable to move forward. And both their business relationship and the business itself are suffering.

What about you? Are you a trustworthy person? Are you really as good as your word? If so, you may find yourself dismayed by people who say they will do something but then don't follow through.

Kate ran into this problem on a fairly large scale. She was the staff member in charge of team-building activities. She helped teams (or silos) arrange quarterly service projects that doubled as team-building events. But the individual silos also wanted to interact with the whole group outside of work hours. When she polled the other members about their interest in having a family night in a large suite at their local ballpark, work teams expressed great enthusiasm. So she collected RSVPs for a particular date, bought the baseball tickets, sent out a "Save the Date" email to staff, and ordered food.

When she sent out a last-minute reminder, the cancellations came rolling in. Three people had forgotten about the game and had made other plans. Some simply did not show up. Kate was beyond frustrated. She was struggling with disappointment about her efforts being wasted and corporate dollars going down the drain.

The frustration of being let down can ruin friendships and divide work teams. And what happens when the failure isn't extracurricular but project-based? It's difficult to measure the loss of both productivity and morale when employees make commitments but don't meet their deadlines. It is situations like these that make managers want to bail out and knock on the doors of "healthier" companies. We've identified four factors that cause people to say yes but not follow through:

1. Insufficient organizational skills or task management skills on the part of invitees. They intend to follow through but there are too many holes in their organizational systems. In this instance, they might forget because they don't have a calendar, they forget to put the event on their calendar, or they put it into their calendar

but they don't set a reminder. They may underperform in a variety of ways.

2. Passive resistance—they didn't really like the plan in the first place but they didn't speak up. They "vote" by not following through.

3. Poor communication or conflict resolution skills. They have trouble telling people "no" and so they overcommit to prevent internal conflict.

4. They may chronically overcommit to things, not realizing that they have too much on their plate.

What can group coordinators like Kate do to get her team to commit to plans and move in the right direction together? Here are some best practices:

Before deciding on a plan of action, try to get input from everyone in a way that feels safe and invites discussion of concerns. You can do this by asking about both pros and cons of an idea. If some people don't speak up, consider taking an anonymous written vote.

Consider potential problems. When making a plan, talk about obstacles that might arise and how you will manage them.

Check the pulse of the group along the way. Ask if they are still on board with you and how they feel as the event approaches. Ask them to reaffirm their commitment.

In summary, everyone feels respected when their views are taken into consideration. Tell your team members that you want them to speak up early in the process about any misgivings they might have. Thank them for their input. In the end, team efforts work better than individual ones. No single person should carry the full load with little appreciation. Everyone should feel engaged, satisfied, and productive.

For Group Discussion

1. *What helps you trust the members on your team?*

2. *What did you do when trust was a problem on your team?*

3. *How did you address it?*

CHAPTER 13

HOW TO REBUILD TRUST

REPAIRING AND REBUILDING TRUST when it has been damaged between people at work can be quite complicated. Even when we have taken action to make things right in a damaged relationship (either through apologizing when we have erred, or in not holding a grudge against someone), we may need to take additional steps to repair the relationship further.

THE THREE PHASES OF BUILDING TRUST

Phase I: Prework

Obviously, the critical question is: "Now what?" There are actually three parts needed to fully answer the question. Before you begin to determine an action plan to rebuild trust, a couple of "prework" steps are needed.

Clarify the situation(s) in which you have a hard time trusting your colleague. Since we have learned that trust is not "all or nothing," when talking (or thinking) about not trusting one of your coworkers, it is helpful to define more specifically:

What is the situation in which you doubt their trustworthiness?

Which aspects of trust (a lack of competence, lack of character or a lack of consistency) lead you to question your colleague's dependability in this situation?

More clearly defining the basis and context for your lack of trust will help you identify your potential action steps. Probably more important, you will more clearly communicate to others what the real issue is for you—either to the coworker, or to someone else directly involved in the situation.

Specifying the situation and the area of concern to you allows for a problem-solving approach to be used. Next, work to increase their competence, or put safeguards in place around concerns such as character or consistency. Otherwise, you and others are stuck with your feeling that you don't trust your colleague. Without taking time to identify the circumstances, source, and level of mistrust, the next step will either be unclear or, more probably, a mistake.

Consider and define your workplace relationship. The next step depends on the nature of your business relationship to the other individual. Do you supervise them directly? Are they a colleague in your department? Is she your supervisor or in a leadership position above you in the organization? Or are they someone you work with, but in a different department or division of the company? The appropriate action to take will be partly defined by the type and nature of your work-based relationship.

Phase II: Implement Guiding Principles

In most important decisions in life, we tend to make better choices when the actions we are considering are filtered through a previously thought-through set of guiding principles. These principles reflect our core values, help us filter out actions that we may want to take in the heat of the moment, and reduce the likelihood of us taking an action that we later would regret.

First, **wait, reflect, observe, and consider before you say anything.** You can't take back your words once you say them. So be cautious before you start.

Second, **be careful about talking to someone else** about your lack of trust in a coworker unless he or she has a direct leadership role in the situation. If you're going to say anything, either talk directly to the other person or talk to your supervisor. Talking about the person to someone else typically leads nowhere positive.

Third, **don't express your concerns in vague generalities.** Give specific examples that illustrate why you lack confidence in the person's competence, a specific character quality, or consistency. If you can't cite any specifics, then you shouldn't raise the issue ("It's just a feeling I have" isn't sufficient).

Finally, **think about specific ways the person may be able to demonstrate their trustworthiness.** Plan ahead and come up with possible opportunities that would let your colleague demonstrate their trustworthiness (or not) in this situation. Then, hopefully, you can reset and move on to another task, and another, and together you can rebuild the trust you have in them.[1]

Phase III: Action Steps to Take When Trust Needs to be Built or Rebuilt

The options for potential actions vary according to the circumstances and "direction" of the trust that needs to be developed. Consider the following.

If you are having difficulty trusting someone else: Most frequently, we are aware of the times and situations where we do not trust someone in our daily work life (we seem to be more cognizant of the pain and tension we are feeling in this type of situation). To improve your ability to work together and move toward a healthier relationship:

- Try to specify, as much as you can, what action you are having trouble trusting them with and why. Ask yourself what they have done or not done to cause this.
- Consider which of the Three C's is related to your lack of trust in this situation.
- Identify situations or actions for which you are willing to trust them. When possible, let them affirm their trustworthiness in these situations.
- Determine what they could do that would shore up your trust of them in this situation and consider certain conditions and parameters under which you would be willing to trust them to do this.

Rebuilding trust (follow-up): You may remember the situation between Nan and Mike described in the chapter on direct communication, when she confronted Mike directly about feeling treated condescendingly in a meeting in front of others. One of the issues stirring up that conflict was the pattern Nan had of expanding projects and taking actions beyond the original parameters of the task. Even after her confrontation with Mike and their working out the respect issue in their relationship, her choosing to take on tasks she was not assigned continued. It became a problem with other team members, both those who were in leadership of the project she was contributing to and with the colleagues with whom she tended to overstep boundaries of responsibility.

The scope of the problem continued to grow to the point that Mike was losing trust in assigning tasks to Nan. He did not want to lose her capabilities and positive contributions to the organization, so he decided he needed to design a process that would manage her more closely *and* provide the opportunity to rebuild his trust in her.

Although she worked on a variety of projects that were underneath the supervision of other senior managers, Mike decided to have Nan report directly to him. First, this gave her an increased sense of being valued (and, in her eyes, a level of prestige)—by reporting directly to the CEO. Secondly, this allowed him to quite clearly and directly communicate what she was being asked to do and *not* to do (at this point in the project, at least). He then set up weekly "check-in" calls to monitor her progress and make sure she wasn't expanding her boundaries on the task, followed up by biweekly in-person meetings.

This "closer supervision" plan worked well. Nan continued to provide excellent value on her tasks, while not overstepping her bounds into other work areas.

If someone is having difficulty trusting you: There are times when someone we work with is struggling to trust us. Rather than feel powerless and give up, we can take specific steps to resolve the situation:

Ask them directly if there is something that you have done that has undermined their trust in you. If so, take appropriate actions like apologizing and making reparations to address this event.

Affirm your desire to be trusted by them and assert your willingness to do what is required to earn or rebuild their trust.

Be willing to take initial actions to demonstrate your trustworthiness, either in other situations or under specific defined parameters.

Be sure to follow through and make evident your competence, consistency, and that you are considering their interests as well as your own.

Building trust in new relationships: When you are new to the work group or you have a new supervisor or colleague, how do you build trust with those who are just getting to know you? When someone is just getting to know us in a work-based relationship, there is reason to be cautious, and trust is not automatic. It makes sense that we have to earn their trust. (An exception to this might be when we have been referred to them and their trust in us is based on the referral's trustworthiness.)

Acknowledge that your new colleagues don't know your capabilities to complete the task successfully and it is reasonable to be cautious initially.

Affirm your trustworthiness to them. Show them you know what you are doing and can complete the task you are committed to doing in the time frame that they need and in the manner they desire.

Frame out the task they want accomplished. Design the project and clarify the goals, expectations, and completion date.

Consider breaking the task into smaller pieces so you can demonstrate your trustworthiness in smaller steps, especially in a new relationship. The other person may be hesitant to trust you for the whole project, and agreeing to a smaller initial phase with subsequent steps may make them more comfortable.

Do the job well, on time, and in the way they expect. In fact, when possible, this is a great time to exceed their expectations— either in quality or completing the task ahead of time.

Working through these steps establishes a trusting relationship with your colleagues, supervisor, or clients. Remember, their initial trust may only be related to a specific project. The way to *broaden* the trust in a relationship is to repeat this pattern for different tasks and demonstrate your various skills, reliability over time, and commitment to do what is best for them. Eventually, you *will* become a trusted and valued colleague.[2]

For Group Discussion

1. *Are you inclined to say yes to too many things at work, just because you want to look like a good team player? What has been the result?*

2. *Do you agree with the idea that you should not talk to a third party (for example, HR) if you don't trust a colleague? Many organizations have procedures in place for this kind of situation. What has been your experience?*

GOING FORWARD . . .

AT THE TIME WE ARE WRITING THIS, much uncertainty is swirling around the world of work—and where that work should actually be accomplished. Many workers have become accustomed to "WFH" and want to continue their remote arrangement. Others prefer a hybrid model. Still others need to be in an office on a daily basis, but want to ditch their long commute for a job closer to home. And in today's economy, they may well find that job. Other employees in various sectors don't have the option of remote work. Retail personnel, health care staff, first responders, some IT professionals, utility workers, and others kept on going all through the pandemic, reporting for work every day.

As HR departments, frontline managers, and senior leadership of organizations large and small think through these challenges, we invite them to also think about the obstacles to healthy communication that exist in today's work world. If companies hire more remote workers, will the teams ever meet in person? There are emotional costs of having employees who are spread out geographically. Friendships are the grease that eases us through challenging workplace conversations. Hopefully, managers will understand the consequences of our shifting work settings and will find innovative new ways to build teamwork and promote harmony. But whether our coworkers are across town or many miles away, it's crucial that video meetings still permit us to resolve relational breaks and rebuild trusting relationships. When team members both know and enjoy each other, projects proceed smoothly and deadlines are met.

What other stressors come with remote work? Employees feel the blurring of boundaries between work and home. One employee quipped, "This is more like living at work than working at home!" Who is bearing the brunt of new workplace stress? In our estimation, it's mid-level managers. They're trying to meet expectations from the top and from their team members. And these concerns are epidemic, including a lack of connectivity between team members and boring, non-useful virtual training.

Additionally, the heat generated by today's political and cultural divides—not to mention the "disinformation" put out on certain media—creates a climate of suspicion and hostility that can spill over into the workplace.

Today, when so many conflicts are "resolved" at the point of a gun or within the anonymity of the internet, we must ask: What would happen if we all learned to resolve conflict more effectively? It's essential that we recognize when our words or behavior have violated the rights of others. When offenses go unacknowledged, the relationship is fractured. The offended party lives with hurt, disappointment, and/or anger. If no one extends an olive branch of peace, the quality of our relationships will continue to diminish. It's essential that we see the humanity in others and respond with love whenever possible.

The same is true in our workplaces—wherever they happen to be.

It is our fervent hope that this book has provided you with a deeper understanding of the sources of conflict and relational breaks—why we or others feel offended, hurt, or disrespected. We also hope that you'll carry with you some practical ways to avoid unnecessary conflict and resolve simple differences. What will happen when these tools are put to use consistently? Employers will see improved employee satisfaction and retention, thereby lowering expenses for hiring and training, team members will shift from clashing with coworkers to working productively on teams, work cultures will grow more positive, and trust will flourish. In short, we hope that you will experience peaceful and productive relationships at work.

APPENDIX

APOLOGY CHEAT SHEET

Things *Not* to Say When Apologizing at Work

When do you tune out of an apology and decide the other person is insincere? Often, we reject an apology as soon as we hear words that blame, excuse, or deny. Do you want to use best practices for apologies that actually work? If so, omit these phrases. When I (Jennifer) am sitting in my consultant chair and I hear these phrases being spoken to a colleague, I often stop the action and say, "You are heading in the WRONG direction. Proceed only if you intend to wreck this relationship with a non-apology."

- Haven't you gotten over that yet?
- I am sorry that you were offended.
- I should be excused because I . . .
- You're too sensitive. I was only joking.
- What's the big deal?
- To the extent that you were offended, I apologize.
- Give me a break.
- You just need to get over it.
- There is nothing I can do about that now. I can't take away the past!

Things *to* Say When Apologizing at Work

What is the right way to apologize? There are two good methods: you could write down the apology and then read it to the person, or you could just say it. Do not try to give a serious apology via electronic media. Taking the time to speak directly with someone better conveys your sincerity.

Here is a useful phrase to help you jump back into an issue: "I'd like to circle back to (name the issue). I realize that I didn't say (or do) things the right way. I apologize for that." This method brings you back to the topic, and it shows your intent to be open and non-defensive.

Next, use some of these tried-and-true apology phrases. Use more than one of these if they really apply to your situation, if the offense has happened repeatedly, and/or if the damage was serious:

- I did it, and I have no excuse.
- I've damaged your trust.
- I was careless, insensitive, thoughtless, or rude.
- I will do the work to fix my mistake going forward.
- You have every right to be upset.
- My mistake is part of a pattern that I need to change.
- I will rebuild your trust by . . .
- I've put you in a very difficult position.
- I realize that talk is cheap. I know that I need to show you how I will change.

Visit 5lovelanguages.com to take the *Making Things Right at Work* Apology Assessment online.

ACKNOWLEDGMENTS

WE ARE INDEBTED TO OUR consulting clients who spoke honestly of their own failures at apologizing and rebuilding trust at work. Others shared the journey that led them to discovering the art of apologizing effectively and finding the success that comes with resolving conflict instead of sweeping it under the rug. This book is enriched by the honesty of these leaders.

We **owe a great deal** to the clients who have turned to us for counsel. Many of the people who have sat in our offices have been there because someone has broken their trust. In their stories, we have seen the pain of rejection and, in some cases, the satisfaction of mending fences. We have changed their names and certain details to protect their privacy, but their stories add much to this book.

We acknowledge that many of the concepts we share in this book are not uniquely ours, but rather a composite of valuable information and concepts we have learned from others over the decades of our professional development—through our graduate training, lectures and workshops we have attended, books and articles we've read, and in conversations with our colleagues. We are thankful for the ability to learn from others and to be able to share those lessons with our readers.

We appreciate the help of Triad Coaching Connection and these individuals: Dr. Nathan White, Dr. Michelle Kane, Elisabeth Bishop, Bill Bishop, and Dr. Jeanne Holmes, who served as sounding boards along the way.

We are also grateful to John Hinkley, Connor Sterchi, Betsey Newenhuyse, Janis Todd, Zack Williamson, and the wonderful team at Northfield, who not only did a superb job in positioning and editing the book but also gave us much encouragement as we did our research and writing.

Finally, we each want to thank our spouses, Karolyn, J. T., and Kathy. Without their love and support, none of us would have had the emotional energy to complete the project. This book is a tribute to their generous spirits.

—GARY CHAPMAN, PhD
—JENNIFER THOMAS, PhD
—PAUL WHITE, PhD

NOTES

INTRODUCTION

1. "Workplace Conflict and How Businesses Can Harness It To Thrive," CPP Global Human Capital Report, July 2008, https://www.themyers briggs.com/-/media/f39a8b7fb4fe4daface552d9f485c825.ashx, 4.

CHAPTER 1: WHY CONFLICT HAPPENS

1. Douglas D. Riddle, Emily R. Hoole, Elizabeth C. D. Gullette, eds., *The Center for Creative Leadership Handbook of Coaching in Organizations* (San Francisco: Jossey-Bass, 2015).

CHAPTER 2: THE FIVE LANGUAGES OF BEING OFFENDED

1. Leigh Branham, *The 7 Hidden Reasons Employees Leave: How to Recognize the Subtle SIgns and Act Before It's Too Late* (New York: AMACOM, 2005), 3.
2. Paul White and Natalie Hamrick, "Specific Acts of Appreciation Valued by Employees," *Strategic HR Review* 19, no. 4 (April 2020), https://www.emerald.com/insight/content/doi/10.1108/SHR-03-2020-0024.
3. Gary Chapman and Paul White, *The 5 Languages of Appreciation in the Workplace: Empowering Organizations by Encouraging People* (Chicago: Northfield Publishing, 2019).
4. Paul White, "Exploring Remote and Onsite Employees' Preferred Appreciation Languages Prior to COVID-19 and during COVID-19," *Strategic HR Review* (July 2021), https://doi.org/10.1108/SHR-04-2021-0017.
5. Gary Chapman and Paul White, *The 5 Languages of Appreciation in the Workplace: Empowering Organizations by Encouraging People* (Chicago: Northfield Publishing, 2019).

CHAPTER 4: THE DANGER OF MAKING ASSUMPTIONS

1. Sandra Graham and Valerie S. Folkes, eds., *Attribution Theory: Applications to Achievement, Mental Health, and Interpersonal Conflict* (New York: Psychology Press, 2014), xx.

CHAPTER 5: THE (HIGH) COST OF INDIRECT COMMUNICATION

1. Gary Chapman, Paul White, and Harold Myra, *Rising above a Toxic Workplace: Taking Care of Yourself in an Unhealthy Environment* (Chicago: Moody Publishers, 2014).

CHAPTER 8: APOLOGIZING IN THE WORKPLACE? REALLY?

1. Everett L. Worthington Jr. and Nathaniel G. Wade, "A New Perspective on Forgiveness Research," in *Handbook of Forgiveness*, 2nd ed. (New York: Routledge, 2020), xx.
2. Karina Schumann, quoted in Sharon Begley, "Why Is It So Hard to Apologize?," *Mindful*, June 2019, 34.
3. Gary Chapman and Jennifer Thomas, *The 5 Apology Languages: The Secret to Healthy Relationships* (Chicago: Northfield Publishing, 2022).
4. Brené Brown, *Rising Strong: How the Ability to Reset Transforms the Way We Live, Love, Parent, and Lead* (New York: Random House, 2017), xx.
5. Quote by Flynn Zaiger, CEO of Online Optimism (a digital marketing firm). Private email conversation between Mr. Zaiger and Jennifer Thomas. Shared with permission.

CHAPTER 9: BEST PRACTICES (AND NOT-SO-GOOD ONES)

1. Harriet Lerner, *Why Won't You Apologize?: Healing Big Betrayals and Everyday Hurts* (London: Duckworth Overlook, 2018), 18.
2. Kieran Corcoran, "Southwest Airlines Apologized for Asking a Woman to 'Prove' Her Mixed-Race Son Was Hers Before Flying," *Business Insider*, May 30, 2018, https://www.businessinsider.com/southwest-apologizes-for-asking-mom-to-prove-mixed-race-son-is-hers-2018-5.

CHAPTER 11: UNDERSTANDING "LETTING GO"

1. Kerry Patterson, *Crucial Conversations: Tools for Talking When Stakes Are High* (New York: McGraw-Hill, 2012), xx.

CHAPTER 12: UNDERSTANDING THE NATURE OF TRUST

1. Jeanne Holmes, Employment Risk Consultant at RiskVersity and adjunct professor at the Fuqua School of Business at Duke University. Private email conversation between Dr. Holmes and Jennifer Thomas. Shared with permission.
2. John C. Maxwell, *The 17 Indisputable Laws of Teamwork: Embrace Them and Empower Your Team* (Nashville: Thomas Nelson, 2001), xx.

CHAPTER 13: HOW TO REBUILD TRUST

1. Maria Elena Duron, "How to Truly Show Appreciation to Colleagues and Clients," U.S. News, February 6, 2014, https://money.usnews.com/money/blogs/outside-voices-careers/2014/02/06/how-to-truly-show-appreciation-to-colleagues-and-clients.
2. Two excellent resources in this area are Stephen M. R. Covey's *The Speed of Trust: The One Thing That Changes Everything* and Paul J. Zak's *Trust Factor: The Science of Creating High-Performing Companies*.

ABOUT THE AUTHORS

GARY CHAPMAN, PhD, is the author of the bestselling The 5 Love Languages® series, which has sold more than 20 million worldwide and has been translated into fifty languages. He is co-author of *The 5 Apology Languages, The 5 Languages of Appreciation in the Workplace,* and forty-five other books. Dr. Chapman travels the world presenting seminars on marriage, family, and relationships, and his radio programs air on more than four hundred stations. For more information, go to www.5lovelanguages.com.

JENNIFER THOMAS, PhD, is a psychologist, author, TEDx speaker, coach, and master facilitator for The 5 Love Languages. She is co-author of *The 5 Apology Languages.* For more information, go to www.drjenniferthomas.com.

PAUL WHITE, PhD, is a psychologist, author, speaker, and consultant, dedicated to "making work relationships work." With Dr. Chapman he is co-author of the bestselling *The 5 Languages of Appreciation in the Workplace,* as well as *Rising Above a Toxic Workplace* and *Sync or Swim.* He is also author of *The Vibrant Workplace.* For more information, go to www.appreciationatwork.com.

We really want to know how you've been impacted by this book. Please email your stories to drpaul@appreciationatwork.com or jen@drjenthomas.com. We look forward to hearing about the difference Making Things Right at Work *has made in your life and the lives of those in your group.*

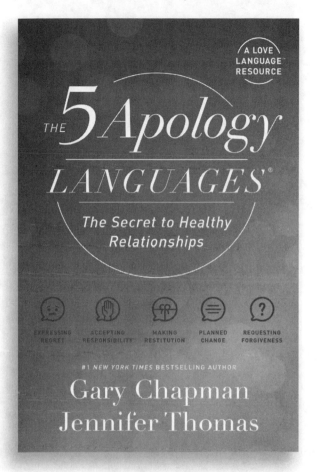

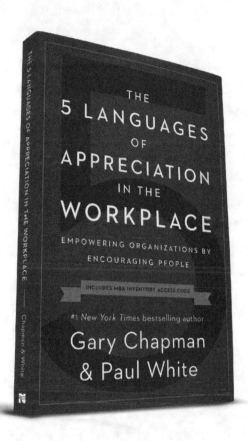

Sam, the new CEO, was ready to hit the ground running—
but his team members had other plans.

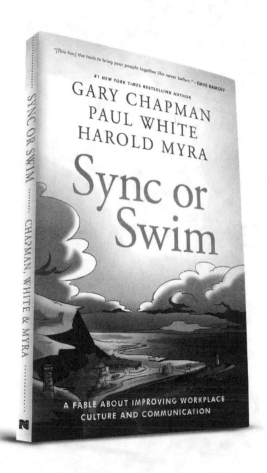

Sync or Swim is a small tale with enormous insight
on ways you can empower, engage, and energize
employees or volunteers facing discouragement
or cynicism. Based on the principles successfully
used by major corporations, health organizations,
over 250 colleges and universities, government
agencies, churches and non-profits.

978-0-8024-2216-3　｜　also available as eBook and audiobook

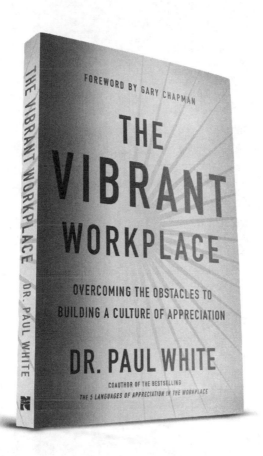

Learn how to thrive in—or escape from—a toxic work environment.